When Lilacs Bloom

Irene Hannon
AR B.L.: 6.5
Points: 5.0

When Lilacs Bloom

Other Avalon Books by Irene Hannon

WHEN THE HEART TAKES WING

WHEN LILACS BLOOM

❖

IRENE HANNON

AVALON BOOKS
THOMAS BOUREGY AND COMPANY, INC.
401 LAFAYETTE STREET
NEW YORK, NEW YORK 10003

PRINTED IN THE UNITED STATES OF AMERICA
ON ACID-FREE PAPER
BY HADDON CRAFTSMEN, SCRANTON, PENNSYLVANIA

To Tom, who makes every day the first day of spring.

Chapter One

"No! I don't want her!"

The speaker rose to his full six feet two inches and glared at the middle-aged man across from him. As he leaned forward and grasped the edge of the desk that separated them, the tightness of his grip turned his knuckles white.

Ordinarily the speaker would have been considered handsome, with naturally wavy, dark-brown hair and a muscular build, but his attractive features had been transformed by anger. His dark-blue eyes blazed threateningly, his cheeks were stained an angry red, a frown darkened his forehead, and his lips were stretched tautly in a thin line. His demeanor would have frightened most people, but the other man was unfazed.

"Will you please sit down and let me finish, Jeremy?" the man asked in a calm, reasonable tone of

1

voice. "At least listen to the idea. You never had a closed mind before."

"Before what?" Jeremy shot back.

"Just before. As in two years ago, when we last had this discussion," the man said patiently. "Don't look for a hidden meaning in everything."

Jeremy stared at the man across from him for a long moment before he straightened up and ran a hand through his thick hair. His shoulders sagged as he relaxed his stiff posture.

"Sorry, Mike," he said, sinking back into his chair. "I thought I was beyond the defensive stage. Go ahead. I'm listening."

Mike gave the man across from him a searching look before he continued.

"Jeremy, you know as well as I do that your work load is far too great. It has been for some time. If you're trying to prove something by denying the need for an assistant, you don't have to, you know. A great deal of the success of this magazine is due to your talent as a photographer. *Journeys* is much more than a typical travel magazine, because you make the stories come alive. You capture the spirit of the people and the places in a way that sets your photography apart, makes it more than 'pretty pictures.' None of that has changed."

"Then why do you want to hire this woman as my assistant?"

"Because, good as you are, two cameras are better

than one. You're doing cover and feature work now, and you simply can't be everywhere at once. You agreed with me when we talked about this a couple of years ago.''

''Things have changed since then,'' Jeremy reminded him.

''Not in terms of your work load. If anything, you're busier now than ever.'' Mike paused, and when he spoke again his voice was softer. ''I thought you'd come to terms with the accident by now. I thought you'd accepted the fact that you've recovered as fully you're ever going to. You have a limp, but it's not incapacitating. It hasn't affected the quality of your work, and I don't expect it to in the future. Your limp doesn't make a bit of difference to me or to anyone else on the magazine.''

Jeremy ran his hand through his hair again, and when he spoke his voice, too, was less strident.

''I know, Mike. Intellectually, at least. But it has changed how a lot of people treat me. I guess I still haven't gotten used to that.''

Mike's eyes narrowed as he regarded the man across from him. He knew Jeremy was thinking of Connie, the fiancée who had deserted him after the accident, when he most needed her support. She had been unable to bear the thought of spending her life with a man she considered a cripple.

''I'm sorry, Jeremy. I know it's been tough. I don't mean to minimize the adjustment, or the pain I know you still have. But your limp has nothing to do with my suggestion about hiring an assistant. It's simply a good business move. There's just too much work for you to handle. One person can't do justice in a reasonable amount of time to the number of stories you cover.''

''But I've always worked alone. I work best by myself.''

''How do you know? You've just admitted that you've never tried working with anyone else. And just think what good experience it would be for a young photographer to work with an acknowledged master of the art of travel photography.''

''Resorting to flattery?'' There was a slight twinkle in Jeremy's eyes.

''Hey, whatever works,'' Mike said with a shrug.

Jeremy gave a brief laugh. ''Okay. Tell me something about this woman you want me to consider.''

Mike smiled. ''Now you're being reasonable.'' He glanced down at a sheet of paper on his desk and adjusted his glasses. ''Her name is Casey Randall. She's worked as a photojournalist for a couple of newspapers, and I was quite impressed with her portfolio. She's won several awards for her pictures, and she has an enthusiasm that will be a great asset in this type of work. I think you should talk to her. She's very good. And with the kind of guidance you can give, she'll get even better.''

"I'm not a teacher. I don't want to waste time on some wet-behind-the-ears journalism graduate."

"Then you won't have to worry about Casey Randall, as you'll see when you look at her portfolio," Mike said matter-of-factly. "I do have some other résumés that you may want to consider, but she seems to be the strongest candidate."

"Well, the work load *is* getting heavier all the time," Jeremy admitted. "It won't hurt to have someone around who can do the more mundane chores."

"Good." Mike looked pleased. "Why don't you take all the résumés with you? I'll leave the selection in your hands."

"Okay, Mike. You win. I'll talk to Casey Randall."

Casey stopped outside the offices of *Journeys* magazine and stared at the imposing entrance. The cold, blustery wind—common in Chicago in March—whipped her coat about her legs, but she wasn't sure if it was the cold or her nervousness that was making her teeth chatter. The realization that she was being considered for a highly coveted position increased her tension, and she closed her eyes for a moment to steady her nerves. So much depended on this interview! She *had* to make a good impression.

With one final deep breath, she pushed open the door and announced herself to the receptionist, who directed her to Jeremy Morgan's office.

As Casey walked down the seemingly endless passage, she took several more deep breaths to steady her pounding heart. She must appear poised and self-confident if she hoped to be selected for this position. And she desperately wanted to be chosen. To work with Jeremy Morgan, a world-class travel photographer, was the chance of a lifetime.

She could thank the managing editor on the daily newspaper where she worked for this opportunity. Apparently sensing that her talents were being wasted in her present job, he had pulled a few strings and arranged an interview for her at *Journeys*. She'd been on her own from there, but Mike Stevens, the editor-in-chief of the magazine, had liked her portfolio, and that had led to this interview. Now if only her luck would hold!

She paused outside the door at the end of the hall, took one more deep breath, and knocked firmly.

''Come in.''

Casey didn't really know what she had expected Jeremy Morgan to look like, but the appearance of the man who rose when she entered surprised her. Mid-thirtyish and devastatingly attractive, he had intense, piercing blue eyes that seemed to cut right through to the heart of a person. No wonder his photographs were so perceptive. She didn't flinch as those penetrating eyes swept over her, but her heart did a strange flip-flop.

''Come in, Miss Randall. I'm Jeremy Morgan.''

She walked toward him and took his extended hand in a firm grasp, noting at this close proximity just how tall he was. He towered over her five-foot, six-inch frame.

''As Mike Stevens probably explained to you,'' he said when she'd sat down, ''I'm thinking about hiring an assistant. He tells me that you're a good candidate for the job. May I see some samples of your work?''

Casey handed him her portfolio, folding her hands tightly in her lap as he studied it in silence. He passed over her early work quickly, but began to look more closely at the photos she'd taken in the past two years.

''How long have you been working as a photographer?'' he asked without looking up.

''Five years. I was lucky to get a job on a small newspaper right out of journalism school.''

He continued to page through the book, and Casey couldn't tell whether he was impressed. His face remained impassive.

''Do you think you could handle the type of work we do here at *Journeys*?'' he asked her suddenly, his razor-sharp eyes locking on to hers. His unexpected question flustered her for a moment, but she quickly recovered.

''I wouldn't be here if I didn't,'' she answered quietly, but with a slight, defiant tilt to her chin. She saw an answering spark of—admiration?—in his eyes.

''This isn't easy work, Miss Randall. Some of our

jobs take us into very remote areas, far from the comforts of civilization. It can be pretty rugged." As he spoke, his eyes swept her slender figure.

"I'm sturdier than I look, Mr. Morgan," she said evenly, holding her temper in check. Casey was all too aware that her fragile appearance was often an obstacle to choice assignments. Her honey-gold hair, shot through with red highlights, softly framed her oval face and hung in long waves down her back. She had been spared the freckles that were the bane of many fair-skinned people, and was blessed instead with a flawless complexion. Her thickly fringed eyes were her best feature, but an elfin nose and lips that were slightly too full kept her from being a classic beauty. Nevertheless, heads always turned as she passed.

Assignment editors had taken one look at her and sent her to cover society events. But her stubborn persistence had paid off, and eventually she'd been given a few other assignments. Her aptitude was soon noted, and lately increasingly substantive assignments had been sent her way.

"If you'll turn a couple of pages . . . there. I went in with the first rescue team to get those shots of tornado victims. Those photographs won a couple of awards."

"Very nice," Jeremy observed. "You obviously do this type of photojournalistic work well. Why switch to travel photography?"

She met his eyes squarely. "Frankly, while I love the interpretive aspect of photojournalism, I'm not sure I'm cut out to cover the kinds of events that make up its heart—natural disasters, crime, that sort of thing. The kind of stories you cover for *Journeys* will let me continue to do interpretive photography, but the subject matter is much more pleasant."

Jeremy looked at her speculatively for a moment and then closed her scrapbook and slid it across the desk.

"You have some nice things in there," he said, making no reference to the answer she had given to his question. "We'll be making a decision within the next day or so, and we'll notify you one way or the other." He stood up, signaling the end of the interview.

As she walked back down the corridor, her spirits took a nose dive. He had given her portfolio no more than a cursory glance. He had been polite, but cool and reserved, throughout the interview. Clearly, she had not made much of an impression.

Oh, well, she thought dispiritedly. She had known from the beginning that this job was a long shot. She'd just chalk the interview up to experience.

Casey was wrong in her evaluation of the interview.

After she left his office, Jeremy sat back down at his desk, a thoughtful frown on his face. Mike had been right. Casey Randall was eminently qualified to do the job—much more qualified than any of the other candidates he'd interviewed. Her pictures were not only technically very good, but they had soul. Certainly, she could improve. Maybe he could help her realize her potential. It was an intriguing idea.

On the other hand, he'd quickly noted that she was not only single, but attractive. Very attractive. She had stirred something in his heart that had lain dormant since Connie walked out on him. The feeling Casey inspired had been a surprising—and disturbing—sensation.

Connie. The very thought of her caused his frown to deepen. She hadn't been able to face life with a cripple. And he really couldn't blame her. With his disability, there was much of her life that he would have been unable to share. In fact, he had come to the conclusion that it would be unfair to ask any woman to make the kind of sacrifices that marriage to him would require. So he'd steeled himself against emotional involvements. He'd been successful so far, but this Casey Randall. . . . It would be dangerous to have her around. If he hired her, he'd have to be very careful or he could find his resolve weakening.

Later that day, after his final interview, Jeremy knew that there was really no other choice. Casey Randall was by far the most qualified candidate. In all fairness, he couldn't give the job to anyone else. With a sigh, he stood up and walked down to Mike's office. "I've reached a decision," he announced.

"Good, good. Who did you choose?"

"Who do you think?" Jeremy said with a shrug. "It was no contest. I'll say this for you, Mike. You can spot talent."

"So. Casey Randall is the one," Mike said, a satisfied smile on his face.

"Casey Randall is the one," Jeremy confirmed.

Chapter Two

Casey paused outside the building that housed *Journeys* and took a deep breath. Once again her heart was racing, but this time it was from excitement, not trepidation. She still couldn't believe that she had gotten the job. Now all she had to do was prove herself. With that sobering thought, she entered the building and headed for Jeremy's office.

"Good morning," he said, looking up when she knocked on his open door. "Mike wants to meet with you first. Sort of an orientation meeting, I suppose. When you're finished with him, come back and we'll get you settled."

Casey flashed him a tentative smile and nodded. He seemed so businesslike and . . . unapproachable. Obviously not the type of person to waste time on pleasantries.

Mike, on the other hand, was very personable and took pains to put her at ease.

"Welcome to *Journeys*," he said with a smile. "Come in and make yourself comfortable."

He discussed the magazine with her, explained the staffing organization, and talked with her in more detail about benefits.

"Any questions?" he asked at last.

"No. Either you've done a very good job filling me in or I'm too new to know what to ask," she said with a smile.

"Well, anytime you want to talk with me about anything, remember that the door is always open."

"I will. And thank you." Casey began to gather up her purse and briefcase, assuming that their meeting was over. But Mike's next words stopped her:

"You know, Casey, the main reason I asked to see you today was that I wanted to tell you a little about Jeremy."

"About Jeremy?" she asked in surprise.

"Yes. I wanted to explain to you about his limp."

"His limp?" she repeated again, frowning.

"You haven't noticed it?" Mike seemed surprised.

"I don't think I've ever seen him walk," she said.

"Well, that explains it. In any case, Jeremy has a rather pronounced limp. It's only natural that you'd be curious about it. He never talks about it, and I'd rather you hear the story firsthand than through the grapevine."

"All right." Casey settled back in her chair, her interest piqued.

"About two years ago, Jeremy was covering a Fourth of July celebration," Mike said. "He was taking photos at a parade when suddenly a little boy darted out into the path of one of the floats. There wasn't time to warn the driver, so Jeremy ran out and pushed the boy clear of danger. He saved his life. But Jeremy wasn't so lucky. He was caught under the float and his leg was crushed."

"How awful!" Casey whispered, her face losing some of its color.

Mike nodded. "For a while the doctors didn't know if they could keep him alive, let alone save his leg. Happily, they were able to do both. But despite their best efforts and months of therapy, Jeremy was left with a limp. And he still has quite a bit of pain on occasion, although he never complains."

He paused, as if choosing his next words carefully. "The bottom line, Casey, is that Jeremy thinks he's come to terms with the limp. And in many ways he has. He certainly hasn't let it affect his career. He's still the best photographer I know. If anything, his work has improved since the accident. He brings back fabulous images, even though it's not as easy for him anymore. As you know, photography can be a very strenuous career."

Casey nodded. "Yes, it can. But it sounds like he's made the adjustment very well."

"As I said, he thinks so. And from a career stand-point, there's no question that he has. But those of us who knew him before the accident are aware of a change. He's much more sensitive about what people say and how they treat him than he used to be. He's more cautious about allowing people to get close to him. He's still struggling with the limp on an emotional level."

"I can understand that," Casey said thoughtfully. "Such a terrible trauma . . . to have your whole life radically changed in an instant."

"Changed more than you might even guess," Mike said. "Before the accident, Jeremy was engaged. Fortunately, his fiancée stuck by him during his recuperation, but when it became apparent that he would never recover completely, that he would always walk with a limp, she broke the engagement. She told him she couldn't bear to live with a cripple."

Casey stared at Mike in horror. "But if she truly loved him, why would a limp make any difference?"

Mike shrugged. "I'm not a psychologist. I'm sure there's an explanation for her actions. Not an excuse, you understand, but an explanation."

"I can't imagine what it would be," Casey said hotly.

"Well, I suppose it's wrong to pass judgment. Perhaps there's more to the story. I just know what Jeremy told me on one of his darker days. I repeat it now only because you'll have to work with him day in and day out, and if you know a little of his background, it may help you to understand him. As you'll probably discover, he's still struggling on some levels to put his life back in order.''

Mike lapsed into a thoughtful silence, giving Casey a few moments to digest his story. How awful to have the one person you love and count on above all others fail you! No wonder Jeremy kept his distance from people. Closeness required trust, and trust implied vulnerability. Jeremy had been hurt too badly in the recent past to take that risk just yet. Closing himself off was a natural protective reflex.

''I hope you'll treat what I've told you as a confidence,'' Mike said at last.

''Of course,'' Casey replied quickly. ''And thank you for sharing it with me.''

''It would have put you at a great disadvantage, going into the situation cold.'' Mike stood up, and when he spoke again, the subject was closed. ''Now, are you ready to get started?''

''I think so,'' she said with a tentative smile.

''Don't worry,'' he reassured her. ''You'll do fine.'' He picked up his phone and pressed a couple of buttons. ''Jeremy? She's all yours. Shall I send her down? Fine.'' He replaced the receiver. ''I hope you enjoy it here at *Journeys*, Casey. I know you'll learn a lot from Jeremy. He's demanding, but he's always fair.''

* * *

When Casey returned to Jeremy's office, he was sitting at the light table. He saw her and motioned her inside.

"So, has Mike indoctrinated you?" he joked.

"It was more a 'welcome aboard' speech," she hedged.

"Then, since you've already been officially welcomed, we can dispense with the formalities and get right to work."

He stood up a little bit stiffly and Casey saw a brief flash of tension pass across his face, as if the motion had been painful for him. As he turned away from her and walked toward a door on the far side of the room, she was aware of his limp for the first time. While obvious, it was clearly not debilitating.

"This used to be a storeroom," he said, unaware of her scrutiny as he flipped on a light in the small room. "But we've converted it into an office for you. I think you'll find everything you need. The entrance is from the hall, but we'll use this door to get back and forth from my office."

Casey glanced into the room. It was small, with a tiny window, and was equipped with a desk, a portable light box for viewing slides, a typewriter, a bookshelf and a comfortable chair. She had time only for a cursory look before Jeremy moved on.

"This is where we store all of the camera equipment,'' he said, removing a key from his desk and opening another door. ''I'll have a key made for you too. Browse around in here this afternoon and see if you're familiar with everything. We have a good selection of camera bodies, lenses, filters, tripods, lights, cases—you can check it out yourself.''

He closed the door before Casey had a chance to give the room more than a sweeping glance.

''Now you need to meet Molly. She does the clerical and secretarial work for me, makes travel arrangements, that sort of thing. You'll be working with her too, of course.'' He led her down the hall and into a large room occupied by a half dozen people, each in his or her own cubicle. Jeremy stopped beside the first office, and a fiftyish, motherly looking woman with gray-flecked brown hair looked up.

''Molly, I'd like you to meet Casey Randall, my new assistant. Casey, this is Molly Clark, who keeps me organized.''

''Welcome to *Journeys*, Casey,'' the woman said with a smile. ''I hope you'll enjoy it here.''

''I'm sure I will,'' Casey replied, responding to the warmth in the woman's tone.

''Molly will fill you in on all the procedural things you'll need to know,'' Jeremy said. ''I couldn't get along without her.''

Molly smiled, clearly pleased by the compliment.

Once he and Casey were back in his office, Jeremy glanced at his watch.

''Sorry to have to run out on your first day here,'' he apologized, ''but I've got a meeting that couldn't be rescheduled. Why don't you settle in your office, check out the camera equipment, and talk to Molly about our procedures for travel?'' He gathered some notes together and placed them in a leather folder as he spoke. ''I should be back by midafternoon, and then I'll answer any questions you have and we can discuss your first assignment.''

''Okay,'' she agreed. Her whirlwind tour had left her a bit disoriented, and she felt her confidence slip a notch.

''You look a little confused,'' Jeremy noted, a brief smile momentarily replacing the slight preoccupied frown he'd worn all morning.

''No, just a bit overwhelmed,'' she admitted.

''It will get better once you're familiar with everything,'' he promised.

Casey watched him leave, realizing with surprise that despite his limp, he moved with an easy grace. He appeared to be in superb physical condition. The muscles in his arms and shoulders were barely hidden by the long-sleeved shirt he wore under a casual sweater vest. She supposed he worked out. Maybe too much, to try and compensate for his lameness.

But she didn't have time to psychoanalyze her boss. She had enough other things to do—such as making a success of this job. She wasn't sure that was going

to be easy. She had a feeling that Mike was right—
Jeremy was going to be a demanding boss.

It didn't take long for Casey to familiarize herself
with her office. It seemed to be well equipped, but
very impersonal. She'd bring a few of her mounted
prints in to hang on the walls. And maybe a plant or
two. That would add some warmth.

On her way to the camera room, she paused to
examine Jeremy's office. Her discerning eye, trained
to look for detail, quickly picked out a few touches
that provided clues to the occupant's personality. Unlike many photographers' offices, Jeremy's was re-
markably neat. The desk held several stacks of papers
and sheets of clear plastic slide file pages, but they
were neatly arranged. The large light table in the
corner also contained slides, but again they were in
well-ordered rows.

Several prints hung on the walls, and Casey examined them curiously. She was surprised to note that
the majority of them were of children, obviously taken
on location shoots. Perhaps there was something
about the essential openness and trust of children that
Jeremy found appealing.

Casey grinned. She was doing it again—playing
psychoanalyst. She'd be better off if she stuck to
photography. She turned her back on Jeremy's office,
resolving to put him out of her mind, and for the next
couple of hours concentrated on doing a survey of the
camera equipment. She was so absorbed in her task

that she didn't hear Molly enter the room until the woman spoke.

"I wondered where you were," the older woman said with a smile. "I was afraid you'd gotten lost."

"Just lost in wonder," Casey said with a grin. "This is fabulous equipment!"

"Jeremy makes sure he has everything he needs. He always says that you wouldn't ask surgeons to operate without the proper instruments, and you shouldn't ask photographers to do their jobs without the right equipment, either."

"Good point. I wish more editors agreed with him."

"Well, it's probably especially important on a publication like *Journeys*. So much of the material is visual."

"That's true," Casey agreed.

"I didn't mean to interrupt you, but it's lunchtime, and I wondered if you'd like to join me. I know Jeremy isn't back from his meeting yet, and since this is your first day I thought you might like some company."

"I'd love some," Casey said.

They spent a pleasant hour chatting in a nearby café, and Casey took a quick liking to Molly. Before the meal ended they had traded background information. Casey had discovered that Molly had been happily married for twenty-five years, had two sons in college, and loved her job. In turn, Casey told

Molly about her family in St. Louis and her brother, Rob, who was a senior in college and planned to go to law school the following year.

"It sounds like you have a wonderful family," Molly said. "But I haven't heard you mention a boyfriend. I should think someone as attractive as you would have the men lined up."

Casey laughed. "Not quite." Then she grew more serious. "I just haven't found the person I want to spend the next fifty years with. You'd think after twenty-seven years someone would have come along, but . . . ." She shrugged. "Maybe my friends are right. Maybe I'm too picky."

"I doubt it," Molly said. "You just know what you want, which is more than I can say for a lot of young people today. Too many people rush into marriage without a second thought. No wonder there are so many divorces." She glanced at her watch and sighed. "Why does the lunch break always go by so quickly? I guess we'd better head back. But let's do this again soon."

"I'd like that," Casey agreed.

When Casey returned to the office she found Jeremy once again at the light table. "Have you had a chance to familiarize yourself with the equipment?" he asked.

"Yes. I've used most of it at one time or another."

"Good. Then we can talk about your first assignment.'' He walked over to his desk and picked up some papers. ''Eventually I'll want you to cover most stories on your own, but we'll do the first couple of assignments together. That way you can see how we operate.''

He handed her a manuscript of about a dozen pages.

''We've got a piece on the Breckenridge, Colorado, ski resort planned for February. That's a copy of the story, which you'll want to read. It's up to us to illustrate it. I think it will be about a five-day trip. We'll leave next Monday. Molly is taking care of the arrangements. Any questions?''

Casey was too overwhelmed by his rapid-fire delivery to do more than shake her head.

''Fine. We'll discuss this in more detail later. Oh, if you ski, bring your equipment along. I'm sure you'll have time for a few runs.''

''That would be great!'' Casey exclaimed, finding her voice at last. ''I haven't skied for a couple of years. Do you ski?''

The minute the thoughtless words passed her lips she regretted them. She saw a flash of pain cross Jeremy's eyes, and a muscle in his jaw twitched. But when he spoke, his tone was conversational:

''I'm sure you've noticed that I have a disability. There are many things that I'm no longer able to enjoy. Skiing is one of them.''

Without waiting for a reply, he turned away and entered the equipment room.

Chapter Three

Casey watched him leave, a sick feeling in the pit of her stomach. How could she have been so stupid? And so insensitive? In her excitement about skiing, she had simply forgotten about his disability.

Now what should she do? Apologize? That would only call more attention to his limp. And it was clear from his carefully controlled tone that he didn't want her to think her remark had bothered him. But she had seen the fleeting pain in his eyes. What a terrible mistake to make the first day on the job. Maybe he was already regretting that he'd hired her.

Slowly Casey rose and walked to her office. She sank into the chair behind her desk and propped her chin in her hand, depression settling over her.

She was still sitting there a few minutes later when Jeremy looked in and asked, ''Do you have a minute to talk about the Breckenridge trip?''

''Of course.'' She jumped up, grabbing a notebook and pen, and followed him back to his office. He appeared to have forgotten their exchange of a few minutes ago, but Casey suspected otherwise. She had seen the hurt in his eyes. Well, she couldn't take back her words, but she could make sure she was never so thoughtless again.

They spent the next hour discussing the trip, and when Jeremy was satisfied that she was well briefed, he leaned back, a slight frown of concentration on his face.

''Okay,'' he said. ''You'll need to do a bit more background work on Breckenridge this week, and talk to Molly about the arrangements. Why don't we get together Friday to discuss our plans, and then we'll leave on Sunday afternoon.''

''That sounds fine.''

Casey spent the rest of the week doing the necessary research and conferring with Molly. She talked at length with the chamber of commerce in Breckenridge to discuss possible photo opportunities, and she set up a number of shots.

Jeremy was in and out of the office a great deal, but he checked with her frequently to make sure that the arrangements she was making were suitable. When it became apparent that she had things well under control, he left her to her own initiative.

By the time they met on Friday, she had arranged the trip down to the last detail.

"I thought that during the day we could concentrate on scenic shots," she said, consulting the note pad in her lap as she sat across from Jeremy's desk. "We also need to get some action shots of downhill- and cross-country skiers and snowmobiling. The evenings will be busy too. There's a skating show on Monday night, a torch run on Tuesday, and a melodrama on Wednesday. On Thursday one of us could take the sleigh ride into the mountains for dinner. We might get some good shots there. And of course one of us will have to visit the local night spots. We can finish up any last-minute shots on Friday."

Casey paused for breath, a small frown on her face as she scanned her list once more. "I think that's it."

"It sounds like you've covered everything," Jeremy said, and the satisfaction in his voice was all the praise she needed. "It looks like we're going to be very busy."

"I think we will be," she confirmed. "At first I thought five days was too long, especially with both of us covering this assignment. But when I started to put the schedule together, I realized that it's barely enough time."

"I see you've booked us on a flight home Saturday morning."

"Yes. I think we'll finish up Friday night."

"But that won't leave you any time to ski."

She shrugged. "I'll go up on the slopes to get some of my shots."

"It's not the same. You'll be so busy checking angles and setting up shots that you won't be able to really enjoy skiing." He picked up his phone and pushed an intercom button. "Molly? Would you please change our return reservations to Sunday about noon? And extend our hotel reservations one night. Thanks."

"Oh, Jeremy, we don't have to stay an extra day just so I can ski!" she protested.

"After the week we're going to put in, you'll need a day of rest and fun," he said. "Besides, if it will soothe your conscience, I'll do a little more shooting that day. So it will be a legitimate workday." He stood to mark the end of the discussion. "I'll pick you up at your place Sunday about"—he glanced at the itinerary she'd handed him—"one? That will give us plenty of time to get to the airport."

"You don't have to pick me up," she said hastily.

He shrugged. "It's not far out of my way. Why take two cars?" She couldn't refute his logic, so she remained silent. "I guess we're set, then," he continued. "You can pack the equipment this afternoon? There's a checklist in the storeroom to follow. I've got to run and I won't be back until late, so just leave everything here by my desk. I'll load it up later."

Casey spent the afternoon packing the camera equipment, double-checking to make sure she wasn't forgetting anything. As he had predicted, Jeremy hadn't returned by the time she left. But everything was in order and waiting for him.

Casey spent Sunday morning packing, emphasizing practicality rather than glamour. She'd spent enough time at ski resorts to know that the ads featuring skintight ski suits and long hair blowing in the breeze were unrealistic. In real life, when the windchills were sometimes far below zero, warmth counted more than good looks.

But although her appearance had never been important to her on prior ski trips, she wished she looked more like the women in those ads. Her navy-blue ski bibs and burgundy down-filled jacket were more practical than attractive. Not that it mattered, she reminded herself firmly. She was there to do a job, not to make heads turn.

She debated the merits of packing any really dressy clothes, but decided against it. She'd been skiing often enough to know that no one dressed up at ski resorts, even in the nicest places.

When Jeremy arrived to pick her up, she was relieved to note that his casual attire matched hers. Boots, dark brown corduroy slacks, and an off-white fisherman's sweater gave him a rugged appearance.

For the first time, Casey became aware of the man's intense masculinity. Why had she never realized before just how incredibly attractive Jeremy was?

"Come in," she said a bit breathlessly, stepping

aside to let him pass and averting her eyes in confusion. What was wrong with her? He was her boss,
for heaven's sake! And she wasn't interested in an
office romance, even if he was—which he clearly
wasn't. In his dealings with her he had always been
polite and professional, if somewhat cool and impersonal. And that was probably for the best.

So why did she suddenly find herself so attracted
to him? She held on to the edge of the door, trying
to still the unexplainable pounding of her heart. She
had never before experienced such a sudden, intense
attraction, and she'd met many handsome men who
were much warmer and more approachable.

Jeremy was apparently unaware of her consterna-
tion. He had entered the room and was looking around
with interest. The walls were painted a restful eggshell
color that complemented the beige carpet. Her couch,
in subtle off-white and beige stripes, blended well
into the room. Accent pillows in grape, rose, and
deep blue added color, as did a chair in deep blue.
A small glass-topped coffee table held a bouquet of
dried flowers in the same shades of grape, blue, and
rose, and a watercolor of a single large iris in pale
blue and green added a fresh pastel touch. Several
stacks of boxes indicated her new-occupant status.

"Very nice," Jeremy commented, his eyes appre-
ciatively completing their survey. "You have a def-
inite eye for color. I've been in some of these four-

family flats before, and most of them are really drab. You've done wonders.''

''Thank you,'' she replied, pleased by the compliment. ''Sorry about the boxes. I'm not quite unpacked yet.''

Jeremy waved her apology aside. ''It takes time. You were lucky to find an apartment in this area.''

''I know. I even have a bit of yard. Look.'' She led the way toward the window and pointed to the tiny patch of fenced ground with its single tree and wrought-iron bench. ''I know it doesn't look like much now,'' she admitted, ''but you have to imagine what it will be like in the spring. The landlord said I could plant some flowers, and then every day I can just look out my window and see a patch of spring. I love to watch for the first buds every year, to see life returning. It never fails to lift my spirits.''

There was silence in the room following her remark, and Casey let the curtain fall back into place with a self-conscious laugh.

''Sorry. I didn't mean to get poetic.''

Jeremy had moved close behind her so he could see out the window, and she turned to look up at him. His eyes, unguarded, held a surprisingly soft, tender look. Casey was thrown off guard. This was not the businesslike Jeremy she knew. Her own eyes widened slightly in surprise, while his suddenly became confused. Abrubtly he turned away and nodded toward her bags.

"Is that everything?" he asked.

"Yes. I've packed only casual clothes." Her voice was slightly unsteady. "I hope that will be all right."

"Fine. What you're wearing right now will probably be standard dress for the trip." His eyes moved over her slender figure, lingering slightly longer than necessary. Or was it her imagination? Certainly her boots, jeans, and Nordic sweater weren't anything to make a man's pulse beat more quickly.

But Casey was wrong. Back lit by the sun streaming in at the window, the red highlights in her hair glimmered like burnished copper, and a faint flush suffused her cheeks with becoming color. Her sweater and jeans emphasized her tiny waist and hinted at the soft curves of her body.

"Ready to go?" Jeremy asked, breaking the electric silence in the room. He stooped to pick up her bags, and she moved quickly beside him.

"I can take one of those." She reached for the smaller of the two bags.

"That's all right. I can manage," he said, and she bit her lower lip. She hadn't offered to take a bag because of his limp, but obviously that was how he had interpreted her suggestion.

"Okay," she said easily, locking the door as they left the apartment. She was on the second floor, and a narrow staircase led down to the front door. Now that she'd been reminded of his limp, she wondered about his ability to negotiate the steps while carrying two heavy bags.

But her concern was unfounded. Although he went down slowly and a bit stiffly, it was clear that he found it no strain. He was obviously used to taking care of himself.

But when they got to the airport it was apparent, even after a porter had been dispatched with the heavier luggage, that more than two hands were needed for the carry-on pieces. Taking a deep breath, aware that she could be asking for trouble, Casey began to pick up some of the camera equipment.

"I'll take care of that," Jeremy said.

"No need. I've got it," she replied, continuing to sling equipment over her shoulder.

"I said I can manage," he repeated, his arm restraining her.

She looked directly into his eyes, and although her heart was hammering, she forced her voice to maintain an easy, conversational tone:

"I'm sure you can. But I'm used to handling my own equipment. I've done it for years. And if we're going to work together, we each need to pull our own weight."

He gave her a searching look, which she returned steadily. It was important that their professional relationship get off on the right foot. It couldn't be one of dependency. It had to be a partnership. And that had to be established now, even if it meant risking his misinterpretation of her action.

Suddenly he relaxed and gave her a small grin. "You win. And you're right. I've just never worked with a woman before. I think I have some learning to do. I didn't mean to imply that you weren't capable."

That was a turn of events! She hadn't intended to give the impression that *she* was insulted. But better to let things rest. After all, she suspected that he had some doubts about her physical ability to handle the job. That was nonsense, of course, and the sooner she dispelled those concerns the better.

"That's okay," she said, dismissing the incident. "Don't you think we'd better board?"

A short time later, as the plane took off, Casey was glad she'd brought a book to read. As soon as they were seated, Jeremy, with a brief apology, set to work making notes and consulting maps for a story he would be photographing in a couple of weeks. This occupied him during the entire two-hour flight. He even continued to work while nibbling on the meal that was served. Not until they were ready to land did he put away his notes.

By the time they collected their luggage, picked up their rental car, and were on the road, the sun was beginning to set. Denver was fairly warm and snowless, and as they left the city and headed into the mountains Jeremy cast a worried eye on the bare slopes. "Looks like they could use some snow here. What's the story on Breckenridge?"

"I called a couple of days ago. They said there was plenty of snow. Once we get through the Eisenhower Tunnel we should see more typical skiing weather."

"You sound like you've made this trip many times."

"Just a couple. I've skied at a few resorts here, but never at Breckenridge."

She wanted to ask him how often he'd skied, but she didn't dare voice her thoughts. However, as if reading her mind, he answered the unspoken question.

"I used to ski quite a bit," he said in a quiet, even voice, as if to let her know that this was not a sensitive subject. "Mostly in Utah and the Sierra Nevadas, and some in Europe. But I hear Colorado is great."

"I've always enjoyed it," she told him. "And I'm looking forward to seeing Breckenridge. It's an old mining town, so it should have lots of character and Victorian charm."

They chatted conversationally for a time, and when they came out of the Eisenhower Tunnel, Casey's prediction came true. They emerged into a full-fledged blizzard.

"Wow," she said, her voice tinged with concern. "I didn't expect the change to be quite this dramatic."

"I think I'd better stop and put on the chains."

There was tension in the air during the last part of

the trip. The swirling snow beat against the windshield and whirled in front of the headlights, obscuring the road, and the hulking, shadowy shapes of the mountains seemed to loom over them in the darkness.

By the time they reached Frisco and made the turn for Breckenridge, the blizzard had subsided somewhat, and Jeremy had proved to be such a competent, skillful driver that Casey relaxed a bit against the back of her seat.

"We're almost there," he said reassuringly, and she flushed to think that her concern had been so apparent.

"I've never enjoyed driving at night or when it's snowing, and when you put the two together . . . . Well, it's a bit nerve-racking," she admitted. "I'm glad you were driving."

He glanced at her, a speculative look on his face, as if unsure whether to take her remark seriously. Clearly he was acutely sensitive to the nuances of words. He started to comment, then seemed to think better of it.

Casey glanced at his profile, dimly visible in the darkness. He was frowning, but whether he was thinking about his disability or simply concentrating on the road, she didn't know. One thing was clear, though. Mike was right. Jeremy still had a long way to go before he recovered from his accident emotionally.

Chapter Four

"We're here."

Jeremy's voice interrupted Casey's thoughts some time later, and she forced herself to focus her attention on the scene ahead. The snow had stopped, and she smiled in delight as they drove down the narrow main street, which was bordered by waist-high drifts.

"Oh, Jeremy, it's charming!" she exclaimed, unable to restrain her enthusiasm. The snow-covered street was lined with quaint Victorian buildings, many painted in pastel tones with gingerbread bric-a-brac in deeper shades. The old-fashioned street lamps, gaily festooned with pine boughs and red ribbons, cast a warm glow over the scene.

Many of the buildings along the street were outlined with tiny white lights in preparation for the Christmas season. Evergreen wreaths with red velvet bows hung on most doors, and Christmas trees twinkled in the windows. Even the newer buildings, interspersed among the historic structures, featured turn-of-the-century architecture.

The sidewalks were populated by laughing groups of people in ski attire, and quick glimpses through the restaurant windows revealed others enjoying good friends and good food.

All the lights and activity were confined, however, to the main street, which was about a dozen blocks long. Beyond that the side streets were in shadows, and the mountains loomed overhead in the background, their outlines dim in the darkness.

Jeremy drove the length of the main street and then pulled over.

"I just wanted to get a first impression of the town," he explained. "I think we passed the turnoff for the inn as we drove through."

"Looks that way," Casey agreed, peering at the map he held. "Why don't you drive and I'll be the navigator?"

"Okay." Jeremy relinquished the map and Casey directed him. When they pulled up in front of the inn a few minutes later, he flashed her a brief smile.

"Well done."

"Thanks. But I don't think I can take much credit. The inn is only a couple of blocks off the main street. Besides, it would be awfully hard to get lost in a town this size," she said with a laugh before turning her attention to the Victorian-style building that was to be their home for the next few days. A sign hung on a wooden post in front, and light shone welcomingly from the windows.

"It looks very cozy," she commented.

"Yes, it does. Good choice."

"Maybe you should reserve your judgment until we see the inside," she warned. "Molly said it was highly recommended by the chamber of commerce, but you never know."

A few minutes later, though, they discovered that the recommendation had been sound. The front desk, of polished oak, was tucked under the staircase and faced the front door. The staircase began on the left and hugged the wall, turning as it went up over the desk, to form a landing.

Just inside the front door on the left was a deacon's bench and an old-fashioned coatrack, and through an arch to the right could be glimpsed a large lounge where a number of people were gathered around a blazing fire. The banister and doorways were decked with green boughs and red ribbons.

"May I help you?" a cheerful voice asked, and for the first time Casey was aware of the young man who had been lost in the shadows behind the desk.

"Yes. We have reservations. Jeremy Blake and Casey Randall," Jeremy said.

The clerk quickly scanned the list in front of him.

"Oh, yes. Rooms six and eight. They're up the

stairs and down the hall. Can I give you a hand with your bags?''

''Thanks, yes,'' Jeremy said.

''Let me help too,'' Casey said, following them out. She saw that Jeremy was about to protest, but he quickly checked himself, and she breathed a sigh of relief.

''My name's Todd,'' the clerk volunteered as he helped them bring in the luggage. ''If you need anything while you're here, either Joan or I will be on duty at the desk. Say, you've really got a lot of photography equipment.''

''We're here to do a photo layout for *Journeys* magazine,'' Jeremy told him.

''That's a great publication!'' Todd said, obviously impressed. ''So this is a business trip? No skiing?''

Casey glanced quickly at Jeremy, remembering his reaction to a similar comment she'd made. But he passed over the remark lightly, saying, ''Casey may do a little.''

After they deposited their luggage in their rooms, Jeremy met her in the hall.

''Why don't we take half an hour or so to settle in and then grab a bite to eat? I don't know about you, but I'm starving.''

''Sounds good.''

''Half an hour, then.''

She nodded and closed the door, turning to examine the room with pleasure. The brass bed was covered with a downy comforter of pale blue, and a matching pale-blue carpet was on the floor. A heavy antique dresser and armoire stood against the walls, which were decorated with brass candle sconces. Hurricane lamps on the bedside table and on the table by the window added a final Victorian touch.

She peeked into the bathroom and was pleased to note that except for the claw-footed tub, it was twentieth century in design.

She unpacked quickly and then touched up her blush and lipstick. No sooner had she replaced her makeup in its case than a knock sounded on her door.

"Ready?" Jeremy asked when she opened it.

"Yes. When you said half an hour, you weren't kidding, were you?"

"I don't kid about eating," he said seriously, but she was caught off guard by the unexpected glint of laughter in his eyes.

"Let's go, then." She reached for her jacket.

"Do you want to walk down to the main street and see what we can rustle up in the way of food? Or would you rather drive?"

"Oh, no, I love to walk through the snow at night."

"A woman after my own heart." He moved aside to let her pass, pulling the door shut behind her.

As they stepped from the lodge, Casey stopped to pull her ski cap over her long hair. They both slipped their hands into warm gloves, and then they headed toward the lights of the main street.

"My goodness, it's dark on these side streets!" Casey exclaimed, her breath coming in frosty clouds.

"Here, you'd better take my arm," Jeremy said, offering it to her. "We can't have you breaking your leg even before you get on the slopes."

"Thank you. I'll take you up on that." She kept her tone friendly but impersonal. But she couldn't stop the delicious tingle of warmth that ran down her spine at his closeness.

She was more aware of his limp now than ever before, for she could almost feel as well as see it. He had developed his own way of walking that was quite graceful and smooth, swinging his right, slightly stiff leg freely, and she fell into step easily beside him.

"Aren't the stars beautiful?" she asked, glancing at the glittering canopy overhead.

"Spectacular," he agreed. "You certainly don't see anything like this in Chicago."

"Have you always lived there?" she asked, and then immediately regretted her impulsiveness. He was such a private person; perhaps he would think she was prying.

"No. I was born and raised in upstate New York," he answered easily, and she breathed a sigh of relief. "My mother still lives there, in fact. But I never really went home again after college. My career always took me to other places. I visit when I can, though, and my sister still lives in the area, so Mom isn't alone."

"That's nice for them. It's good to have family close by."

"Your family is in St. Louis, right?"

"Yes. Close, but not close enough," she said with a sigh.

He didn't comment on her remark. Instead, they walked in silence to the main street and quickly chose a place to eat.

"We can be more selective later in the week. Right now, anything would look good," Jeremy said, and Casey concurred.

While they ate, they discussed their plans for the next day. Casey agreed to get some downhill shots on the slopes while Jeremy concentrated on snowmobiling. They also divided up the evening assignments.

"Let's plan to have breakfast together every day, and dinner, if possible," Jeremy said as they walked back. "But otherwise we'll have to go in different directions. There's just too much to cover."

"I agree. We'll be busy enough alone—we'd never get everything done if we stayed together."

That was the way the week passed. They had an early breakfast, and then they parted. Casey got in some skiing while doing her shots of downhill skiers, but Jeremy had been right. It wasn't like skiing just for fun. She was glad he'd added the extra day so she could really enjoy the sport.

Between the two of them, they'd covered all but one of the items on Casey's list by the end of the week. But they didn't even have time to eat dinner together most days. And Casey fell into bed exhausted every night, often without even seeing Jeremy.

By Friday night, the only place neither had visited was a quaint Victorian restaurant on Casey's list. They discussed this over dinner.

"I called the owner today, and we've got permission to shoot there tonight if we want to," Casey said.

"Good. Let's head over there as soon as we're finished."

The restaurant was as pleasingly old fashioned as promised, and for once Casey and Jeremy worked together to get the shots that best captured the atmosphere of the place. The going was slow, however, because they were constantly being interrupted by friendly but curious diners.

When at last they put away their equipment, it was after ten. Casey was exhausted by her long hours, physically demanding assignments, and the constant exposure to the frigid air. She felt as if she could sleep for a week.

"Are you all right?" Jeremy's concerned voice penetrated her weariness.

"Of course." She summoned up a smile, loath to admit her tiredness. He'd had doubts about her stamina from the beginning, and she didn't want to do anything to confirm those doubts.

"We've kept up a pretty grueling pace for the last week," he admitted. "I'm beat. Most of the trips aren't this bad. I usually try to take some evenings off, or else some time during the day."

"I'm fine, really. I expected to be busy."

"Well, let's head back to the inn and get a good night's sleep. You've got a full day of skiing ahead of you, so you need some rest."

Casey groaned inwardly. The idea of facing the slopes for a strenuous day of skiing tomorrow didn't appeal to her. She would much rather curl up by the fire with a good book and some hot chocolate. But it had been thoughtful of him to arrange it, and she felt obliged to take advantage of the opportunity.

The next morning she didn't feel much more enthusiastic, but she forced herself to be cheery. Maybe she would be more excited when she was out on the slopes.

And she did feel much perkier once she started her first run. The sky was an incredible deep blue, the snow was brilliant white, the deep green spruce trees were laden with white powder puffs of snow, and the pure, clean air was invigorating. This had been a good idea after all.

As she began her descent, falling quickly into the familiar, easy rhythm of poling and parallel turns, she felt herself relaxing. She supposed she'd been under more pressure than she'd realized this last week, working harder than necessary, anxious to prove herself. It felt good to forget about all that for a few hours.

As she neared the end of her final run of the day, she paused for a moment at the top of the last slope that led to the base lodge. She saw Jeremy in the distance, a camera around his neck, and she raised her pole in greeting. He responded with a wave, and then she turned her attention back to the slope. Concentration was always important in skiing, but especially so at the end of the day when one was growing tired. Mentally preparing herself, she pushed off onto the final stretch of moguls, skillfully negotiating the tricky bumps. When at last she made a quick, clean stop next to Jeremy, he gave her an appreciative smile.

"Nicely done. You're very good."

She flushed with pleasure. "Thank you. I'm afraid I'm a bit rusty. It's been awhile since I skied."

"You'd never know it. That last run was difficult, and you handled it very well."

"I have to admit it was challenging," she said with a smile as she unsnapped and stepped out of her skis. Before she could protest, Jeremy reached down and swung them easily to his shoulder. As if reading her mind, he held up his hand.

"I know, I know. You can handle them. I believe you. But when we're not working, let me be a gentleman, okay? This is what my mother taught me to do, and I wouldn't want to disappoint her."

When he had that pleasant, cajoling smile on his

face and his tone was so warm, Casey didn't have the heart to protest.

"Thanks," she capitulated with a smile. "I must admit, carrying skis is not my favorite part of skiing. They're so awkward, especially when you're trying to walk in these," she said, indicating her boots. "They're so heavy and clunky."

Jeremy laughed, an easy, unforced laugh, and Casey began to realize what a charming man he could be. Was this what he'd been like all the time before the accident?

"I remember," he said, with no trace of bitterness. "I was always amazed at how graceful they were on the slopes, though. They just aren't designed for walking."

Jeremy stepped aside to let Casey enter the ski-rental shop, and she sank down on a wooden bench.

"Boy, am I pooped!" she admitted, leaning back against the wall. "Skiing looks so effortless, but until you try it you don't realize how much work it really is."

"True." Jeremy nodded, bending down to unhook her boots and gently pull them off her feet. She smiled and wiggled her toes as he did so.

"That feels good," she said.

She slipped her own boots on while he turned in her rented equipment, and was ready to leave by the time he reappeared.

"All set?" he asked.

She nodded, and when he offered her his arm she took it without a second thought, falling into step beside him as they started back to the inn. Somehow, with her arm in his, she felt inexplicably happy. It must be due to an exhilarating day of skiing and a successful first assignment, she decided.

"I thought we might eat at the restaurant we photographed last night," he suggested. "It was very nice, and the food looked good."

"That would be great! I'm starved."

"What did you have for lunch?"

"I must admit that I was having so much fun skiing I didn't even stop to eat."

"You mean you haven't had anything since breakfast?"

"No."

"Well, we'll make it an early dinner, then. Why don't we freshen up and then head over to the restaurant about five-thirty?"

"That would be fine."

Jeremy left her at her door, and Casey headed for the bed like a homing pigeon. She was thoroughly exhausted, and she wanted to stretch out for just a few minutes.

The next thing she was aware of was a persistent knocking. With a frown she sleepily opened her eyes, but the room was dark. Suddenly her eyes flew open and she glanced at her watch. Five-thirty! She'd been asleep for an hour and a half!

Quickly she scrambled off the bed and padded to the door, brushing her hair back from her face. What was she going to say to Jeremy? She hesitated, frowning, her hand on the doorknob. But there was no way out. She had to face him. Taking a deep breath, she opened the door.

"Finally." Relief tinged his voice. "I was just about to call. Are you all right?" he asked in concern, noting her disheveled appearance as the light from the hall illuminated her figure.

"Yes," she said with an embarrassed smile. "I'm sorry, Jeremy. I fell asleep. No excuses. If you'll give me five minutes, I'll meet you in the lobby."

"Don't rush. If you'd rather not go out . . . ."

"No, of course I want to go. I should have set my alarm, but I never dreamed I'd fall asleep."

"It's okay," he assured her. "Take your time. I'll wait for you downstairs."

Despite his reassurance, Casey flew about the room, quickly running a brush over her hair and repairing her makeup. She was downstairs in less than the promised five minutes.

"That was quick," Jeremy said with a surprised smile rising as she entered the large lounge.

"Chalk it up to hunger," she replied with a laugh.

"And I thought it was my irresistible company," he said with mock chagrin.

Casey looked at him curiously. She'd never heard him tease with quite that uninhibited tone before, and she was delighted to discover that he had a quick wit and a sense of humor. What other surprises did he have in store for her?

They walked quickly through the cold night air, their boots crunching on the snow, her arm once more tucked into his. Their breath made frosty clouds, and both seemed reluctant to break the deep stillness of the night, content to enjoy the peaceful silence.

They arrived at the restaurant within minutes and were greeted by the smiling hostess who had been on duty the night before.

"Back again?" she asked.

"Yes, but this time for pleasure, not work. We want to sample some of the delicious food we saw last night."

She led them to a cozy table for two near a window. A candle burned in the center, casting a warm glow on the old-fashioned wallpaper and pewter plates.

"This is absolutely charming," Casey said, biting into a warm homemade cinnamon roll from an assortment quickly provided by the waiter. "It's a perfect way to end the trip."

"I agree. A charming restaurant and a charming companion," he said lightly, placing his napkin in his lap.

Casey was saved from having to respond to this unexpected compliment by the timely appearance of the waiter.

While they dined on salad, corn chowder, brook

trout, baked potatoes, and homemade chocolate-cream pie, the conversation rambled over a number of topics. Casey learned that Jeremy enjoyed such sports as sailing, swimming, horseback riding, and archery.

He also lifted weights, a fact that didn't surprise her. No one could have a physique like that without working at it. He wasn't overly muscular, but she knew that there wasn't an ounce of fat on his hard, lean body. If his intention had been to prove that a lame leg was no excuse to be physically unfit, he had definitely succeeded.

They discussed politics, literature, and current movies, and Casey found that they shared similar views on many subjects. The evening passed more quickly than she would have believed possible. Two weeks ago she would not have looked forward to a whole evening in the company of businesslike Jeremy Morgan. But now she was enjoying herself thoroughly.

As he took the last bite of his dessert, Jeremy leaned back, a relaxed, contented look on his face.

"After that meal, I think a walk is in order," he announced. "Are you too tired?"

"No. But I'm so full I don't know if I can even stand up, let alone walk."

"You'll feel better after we start moving," he promised, and he was right. As they strolled down the colorfully lighted main street, her arm tucked protectively in his, she realized that she was sorry to see the trip draw to a close. Jeremy had proved to be an unexpectedly pleasant, interesting, and thoughtful companion.

But all good things have to end, she thought ruefully as they headed back to the inn. The evening wasn't over yet, though.

"How about a cup of hot chocolate by the fire?" he suggested when they entered the inn.

"That sounds wonderful," she agreed readily, glad to have an excuse to extend the evening, despite her tiredness.

And so they sat side by side in the flickering firelight, enjoying steaming mugs of rich hot chocolate.

"Mmm, this is heavenly," she said with a smile, closing her eyes as she leaned back against the couch. "I think I could stay here forever. Couldn't you?"

When he didn't respond after a few seconds, Casey opened her eyes lazily to find Jeremy gazing at her intently. When he realized that she was watching him, he turned away and stared into the fire, grasping his cup in both hands as he leaned forward. She thought perhaps he hadn't heard her, but she was mistaken.

"Yes," he said. "I haven't been this content and happy since . . . for a long time." He drained his cup quickly and stood up. "I think it's time we both got some sleep."

Casey hastily finished her hot chocolate and then

they made their way up the stairs. Though they were not touching, the air seemed charged with electricity.

When they reached her door, she fitted the key into the lock and then turned to face him, not knowing what to expect.

For several long seconds he just looked at her, and she tried to read his thoughts in his eyes. He seemed troubled, but she must be wrong. What was there to be troubled about? They'd had a lovely evening.

"Good night, Casey," he said abruptly. Then, before she could respond, he turned and walked away.

Chapter Five

After that disquieting parting, Casey thought that sleep would be elusive. But she was more tired than she realized, and she quickly fell into a deep slumber.

The next morning, however, she awoke with a scratchy throat and a general feeling of malaise. *This is great*, she thought. Just what she needed. *Well, maybe the sore throat will go away*, she thought hopefully, deciding to ignore it as much as possible.

She joined Jeremy downstairs for breakfast, noting that the warmth he'd exhibited during dinner the previous evening was noticeably lacking.

"Good morning," he said politely, "Would you like some coffee?"

"No, thanks. I'll just have juice and toast."

"That's a pretty lean menu."

"Well, I'll be sitting most of the day, and that doesn't require many calories."

"You don't look as if you have to worry about calories."

"That's because I do worry about them," she said with a smile, and though he made no comment, she was please to note that her remark brought a glint of laughter to his eyes.

Even the toast was too much for her rapidly worsening throat, however, and she simply crumbled it into small pieces. She was afraid Jeremy would notice that she wasn't eating, but if he did, he made no comment.

Conversation in the car lagged during the drive back to Denver, and Casey wasn't sorry. It hurt to talk. Jeremy seemed to be deep in thought much of the time, so she made no attempt to break the silence.

There was no time to talk in the airport, either, as they attended to the business of returning the car and checking the bags. And once on the plane, Casey found her eyes growing heavy.

She had never been able to sleep on planes, but to her amazement she slept soundly until she felt her shoulder being gently shaken. Sleepily she opened her eyes, only to discover, to her horror, that her head was nestled on Jeremy's shoulder. Quickly she straightened up, brushing her hair back from her face.

"I'm sorry," she said, her cheeks hot.

"No need to be. My shoulder wasn't doing anything else." He gave her a quick grin.

By the time they reached her apartment, she was

feeling too ill to protest when he carried her bags up the stairs. She was glad he didn't linger, and as soon as she shut the door behind him she headed for her bedroom, not even bothering to change clothes or unpack. She stopped only long enough to take two aspirins. As soon as her head hit the pillow, she fell into a fitful sleep.

When Casey awoke, slightly disoriented, her room was dark. With a frown she glanced at her watch, struggling to focus on the illuminated hands. To her surprise she discovered that it was two in the morning.

She forced herself to get up and put on pajamas, splashing cold water on her flushed face and taking two more aspirins. She knew that she was running a fever, but there wasn't much she could do about it in the middle of the night. Wearily she climbed back into bed, setting her alarm for six.

She needn't have bothered, however, because she tossed and turned the rest of the night, alternating between being too hot and too cold. When at last it was time to get up, she seriously considered calling in sick. But she couldn't do that. It would only confirm Jeremy's doubts about her stamina.

She swung her feet to the floor and stood up, holding on to the wall for a moment until the room steadied. Her whole body ached and her throat was raw. How was she going to make it through the day in this condition?

Gritting her teeth, she forced herself to get dressed.

She considered eating, but the thought of food turned her stomach. All she'd had in the last thirty-six hours was a few bites of toast, but she knew that today she couldn't even tolerate that.

She reached the office before Jeremy, but she heard him come in a few minutes later. Shortly after his arrival he walked into her office.

"I've got an appointment this morning, Casey. Would you put the equipment away and send out the film for processing?"

"Of course," she said with a smile, amazed at the tremendous effort it took to respond.

"Say, I think you've got a touch of sunburn," he remarked, his eyes on her flushed face.

"Could be," she said. "The sun's pretty intense up there."

"Well, I'll be back early this afternoon." He left, and she heard his footsteps retreating.

Casey was never quite sure how she made it through the morning. She mechanically did the tasks Jeremy had asked her to do, but it took her longer than expected. She also had to handle a number of phone calls, two of which required some research. She was on her knees putting away the last of the equipment when Jeremy returned.

"Did you send the film off?"

His unexpected appearance in the equipment room startled her, and she stood up quickly, grasping the cabinet as she did so.

"Oh! Yes. It went out first thing." She was finding it hard to concentrate, and Jeremy seemed to be wavering slightly.

"Good. I'm eager to see what we got."

Casey heard his words through a fog. The room seemed to be tilting strangely, and she took a firmer grip on the cabinet.

Jeremy suddenly seemed to realize that there was something wrong, for he took a step toward her.

"Are you all right?" he asked with a frown.

"Yes. I'm fine," she said, but her voice broke betrayingly. Before she knew what was happening, he was beside her tilting her chin up and looking into her eyes, a frown on his face. A cool hand was placed against her forehead, and she heard him mutter something under his breath.

"You're burning up! How long have you been sick?" he demanded.

"I woke up with a scratchy throat yesterday," she replied, too sick and weary to fend off his questions. "It was worse today."

"I'll say. Why did you come in? Have you called a doctor?"

"I didn't want to miss a day so soon after starting. And I don't know any doctors here," she said, close to tears. She mustn't cry, she told herself fiercely. He would only consider that a sign of weakness.

Suddenly, realizing how close she was to collapse,

Jeremy changed his tone. Gently he placed an arm around her shoulders and guided her into his office.

"I'm taking you home," he said firmly but gently. "You should be in bed. Then I'm going to call my doctor. He can send something right away. And no protests," he warned when she started to speak.

Mutely, Casey allowed him to take charge. She was too ill to put up a fight. As he helped her on with her coat, Molly knocked and came in.

"Here are the files you asked for, Jeremy. Casey, what's wrong?" she asked in concern, noting Casey's flushed face and dull eyes.

"She's sick. I'm taking her home," Jeremy said shortly.

"You poor thing. I wondered why I hadn't seen you all morning." She placed a motherly hand on Casey's forehead and shook her head. "You've got a high fever." She gave Jeremy a worried look. "See that she stays warm and goes right to bed."

"I will."

Casey let him lead her out of the building, grateful for the strong arm that helped support her. She couldn't remember ever feeling this weak and disoriented before.

When they reached her apartment, Jeremy helped her into the bedroom. She sank gratefully onto the bed, her shoulders drooping.

"Can you manage to change and get into bed?" he asked her.

She nodded, not at all sure it was true. But she wouldn't put it past him to stay and help her get undressed, if necessary. Not that he would treat her in anything but a brotherly manner. It was *her* reaction that worried her. Her heart seemed to do unexplainably strange things in his presence. It was a ridiculous reaction, she knew, for he'd certainly given her no encouragement. To him she was strictly a business associate.

Although his eyes registered doubt at her nod, he didn't argue. "All right. Do you have a thermometer?"

"I think so. It's in the medicine cabinet." She started to rise, but he pushed her gently back onto the bed.

"I'll get it. You change while I'm gone." He walked out of the room, shutting the door quietly behind him.

She closed her eyes, trying to still the throbbing in her head. She could hear Jeremy rummaging around in the medicine cabinet. She ought to get up and change, as he'd told her to do, but she was gripped by an intense lethargy.

The noise in the bathroom ceased abruptly, and then she heard him opening cabinets in the kitchen. A faucet was turned on. A glass was being filled. Concentrating on those sounds helped her keep her mind off her throbbing temples.

"How are you doing?" Jeremy called through the door.

She put her hands to her head and closed her eyes. She hadn't moved since he'd left. "I haven't changed yet."

"Can I come in?"

"Yes."

He pushed the door open and frowned when he saw her.

"What's wrong? Why are you still sitting there?"

"I'm sorry. I'm just so tired, and my head hurts," she said, a sob catching in her throat.

Jeremy put the thermometer, a glass of water, and a bottle of aspirin on the bedside table and sat down beside her. Silently he gathered her into his arms as if she were a child, gently stroking her hair.

"It's okay, Casey. Everything will be fine. You just need some rest."

She clung to him gratefully, taking comfort in the solid warmth of his presence. She was frightened by this illness, which seemed to have drained her of every ounce of energy, and it was good to know that she was not alone. But concern for his health caused her at last to push against his arms.

"Jeremy, I don't want to give you this," she protested. "I'll change now, if you'll wait outside."

"Are you sure you can manage?"

"Yes."

"Okay. I'll be just outside the door if you need me."

She was all too much aware of Jeremy's presence on the other side of the door as she changed into a flannel nightgown as quickly as her shaking fingers would allow. Knowing that he would take charge if she couldn't accomplish the task gave her the incentive to find the necessary energy.

She was afraid he would get impatient, but he waited until she had climbed into bed, pulled up the covers, and called "come in" before he entered.

"That's better," he said approvingly as he sat beside her and pulled the thermometer out of its case. "Open up."

She did as instructed, and he shook out some aspirin and adjusted the covers while they waited for her temperature to register. Casey was deeply touched by his concern, and her heart ached with an unfamiliar longing. She didn't understand what was happening to her, and she was too ill to try to figure it out now. Instead, she closed her eyes.

After a few minutes, Jeremy moved back beside her and removed the thermometer, frowning as he read it.

"Well?" she prompted.

"One hundred and three." He shook it down and looked at her. "You are one sick lady. I'm going to call the doctor right now."

She could hear him talking on the phone in a low

voice in the next room, but she couldn't distinguish his words. Not that she tried. It would have required too much of an effort.

"The doctor prescribed some medicine, and I'm going to run out and get it. There's a pharmacy down the street," he said, returning more quickly than she expected. "Will you be all right alone for a little while?"

"Of course. But I don't want to put you to any trouble. You've done enough already," she said miserably. He was probably sorry now that he'd ever hired her.

"It's no trouble. Get some rest while I'm gone."

Casey fell into a restless sleep almost as soon as Jeremy left. She didn't hear him return, but a gentle shaking aroused her. She opened her eyes in confusion, thinking for a moment that she was back in Colorado. Was it time to do some more shooting? She didn't want to go back out into the cold.

Suddenly Jeremy's face came into focus above her, and she sent him a wan smile as memory returned.

"Hello," she whispered.

"Hi. I got the medicine." He held up two bottles. "I'll get some water."

He disappeared through the door, returning a few moments later with a glass.

"You're supposed to take two of these every four hours and one of these every eight hours," he said, reading the labels on the bottles. He unscrewed the caps and shook out the correct number of tablets.

Casey struggled to sit up, but it was too much of an effort. Realizing her predicament, Jeremy quickly slid an arm around her shoulders and supported her, holding the glass to her lips. She had difficulty swallowing the pills because her throat was so swollen, but at last she managed it. Then Jeremy lowered her back to the bed and tucked the blankets around her.

"The doctor says that if you're not drastically improved within twenty-four hours, he wants to see you. Now get some sleep." He rose and walked across the room, seating himself in a small overstuffed chair by the window.

Casey looked at him in surprise. "What are you doing?"

"I'll stay for a little while."

"You don't have to do that. I'll be okay. I know you have things to do at the office."

"They'll wait. Don't worry. Just rest."

She could see that he wasn't going to budge, so she gave up trying to convince him. But she was sure that she would never be able to sleep, knowing that he was sitting so close by watching her.

The medicine did its work, however, and in a few minutes she found herself drifting to sleep. Soon she had fallen into a heavy slumber from which she found it hard to awaken when she felt someone shaking her shoulders and calling her name four hours later. Why didn't whoever was bothering her leave her alone? She shut her eyes tightly and frowned in annoyance, restlessly pushing her damp hair back from her face. She was so hot! She flung the covers back and mumbled, "Leave me alone."

Instead, she felt the covers being drawn back up and tucked firmly under her chin.

"Come on, Casey. Wake up," a voice coaxed. "It's time to take your medicine."

Groggily she gave in, only vaguely aware of Jeremy's worried face above her. He once again put his arm around her and helped her to a sitting position, holding a glass to her lips as she struggled to swallow the pills he placed in her mouth. When she succeeded, she was eased back to the pillow, and darkness closed around her again.

This scenario was repeated four hours later, and Casey was again too groggy to be really aware of what was happening. But two hours later, when she awoke shivering, her nightgown damp with sweat, she knew that her fever had broken. She was no longer hot, but she was so weak that she could barely move. At least her mind was functioning coherently now. She frowned at her watch—almost midnight! Suddenly a shadowy figure rose out of the corner, and Casey's eyes widened in alarm.

"W-who's there?" she whispered.

A soft light was flipped on, and Casey's mouth dropped open when she recognized Jeremy.

"Jeremy! Why are you still here?" she asked incredulously.

He moved over and sat beside her, taking her hand in his.

"You weren't in any shape to be left alone," he said matter-of-factly. "Besides, you needed someone here to give you your medicine." He placed a hand on her forehead. "I think your fever is gone."

"It is," she confirmed, shifting uncomfortably in her damp nightgown.

Sensing her discomfort, he reached to her shoulder and felt the flannel material.

"You need to change. Where do you keep your pajamas?" he asked, rising and glancing toward the chest of drawers.

"Second drawer from the top. But I can manage," she protested, unwilling to have him rummaging through her lingerie. He ignored her protest, however, and quickly selected another long flannel gown.

"How's this?" he asked, holding it up.

"Fine. Just leave it on the bed."

"I'll make some tea while you change."

As soon as he was out of the door Casey rose, but her shaky legs wouldn't support her. She quickly sank back onto the bed and awkwardly changed in that position. As she did so she caught a glimpse of herself in the mirror over the dresser. She stared at the reflection, hardly recognizing the pale face, deeply shadowed eyes, and tousled hair. She pushed distractedly at the limp strands, but it was hopeless.

"Okay?" Jeremy called through the door.

"Yes," she replied, with a last disheartening glance in the mirror.

Jeremy entered with a cup and saucer, which he set carefully on the bedside table. Then he turned and silently gave her a thorough scrutiny. She lowered her eyes, uncomfortably aware that his razor-sharp eyes, trained to observe detail, probably missed nothing during this appraisal.

"I know I'm not Miss America," she joked at last to break the silence, uncomfortably aware of the accuracy of the statement.

He dismissed her comment with an impatient shake of his head. "The important thing is that your fever broke. But you must be feeling better if you're worried about your appearance. Now let's get you back into bed."

Once she was in bed, he handed her the cup and saucer.

"Drink this tea. You need some fluid in your body," he said, then seated himself again in the chair by the window.

"I can't thank you enough for your concern, Jeremy," she said as she sipped the steaming liquid. "I don't know what I would have done without you. I didn't even have the name of a doctor to call."

"I'm glad I was able to help."

She looked at him over the rim of her cup as she drank, and a deep ache of tenderness welled up inside her. He had long since loosened his tie and discarded his jacket, and his shirt was wrinkled. His thick hair, usually neatly combed, was tousled. This was a side of Jeremy Morgan she'd never seen before. He was always so perfectly groomed. Yet in this rumpled state he looked endearingly vulnerable.

She wondered again what he had been like before his accident. There had been moments—on the ski trip and right now—when she felt as if she were getting a glimpse of the real Jeremy, but they were always fleeting. He had insulated himself too well to allow anyone to get too close. She only hoped that someday he would learn to trust again.

When she finished her tea he rose and took the cup.

"Now go back to sleep and rest," he instructed her.

"I will. But there's no need for you to stay. It's after midnight, and you have to go to work tomorrow. I'll be all right now, really."

He stared down at her, a frown on his face. She could tell that he was undecided, so she pressed her advantage.

"Jeremy, be sensible. My fever is gone. I can take my own medicine. And if you stay up all night, you'll be exhausted tomorrow. Your resistance will be down, and you might get sick. *Journeys* can get along without an assistant photographer for a few days. But you've got too much going on in the next couple of weeks to risk being sick.''

Her logic was irrefutable, and she knew it. But he seemed reluctant to accept it.

"I don't know," he said, shaking his head. "I'm not sure you should be left alone."

"I'm much better. And I promise to set my alarm so I won't forget to take my medicine. There's really nothing you could do if you stayed, except get more tired. I'm sure I'll just sleep the rest of the night. And you must be starved!" she said, suddenly realizing that he hadn't left her long enough to eat.

"I must admit that I raided your refrigerator," he said with a slightly sheepish smile. "Although there wasn't much to raid. I scrambled a couple of eggs."

"I tried to clean it out before our trip," she apologized. "I was afraid things would spoil. Well, I'll owe you a dinner."

"I was just kidding."

"I insist. As soon as I get back on my feet, I'll cook you a gourmet feast to make up for today. And that brings me back to the point. Please go home and get some rest. I feel bad enough about imposing on you as it is."

He rose reluctantly. "Okay. But be sure to take your medicine. And I'll leave my home phone number in case you need anything." He withdrew a small notebook from his pocket and jotted down some numbers. Then he tore off the slip of paper and placed it on her bedside table. ''Don't hesitate to call.''

''I won't. And thank you again, Jeremy. I'm sorry I was so much trouble.''

He reached over and, for a fleeting instant, gently touched her cheek.

''You were no trouble, Casey,'' he said softly. ''Sleep tight.''

Chapter Six

The dissonant, persistent buzzing of the alarm clock roused Casey from her deep slumber twice, and she dutifully but sleepily swallowed her pills each time. The next time her sleep was interrupted, the telephone was the culprit, and she opened her eyes to the dazzling brilliance of a cold winter morning. A glance at her watch told her it was nine o'clock.

At first she considered ignoring the phone. She was too cozy under the blankets, and the air in the room was decidedly chilly. But the phone just kept on ringing. At last, with a sigh, she gave in, swung her feet to the floor, and shrugged into her robe, wrapping it tightly around her for warmth. She still felt very weak, but at least her fever was gone and her throat was only slightly sore. Whatever Jeremy's doctor had prescribed had certainly done the trick.

She half suspected that by the time she reached the

telephone whoever was on the other end would have grown impatient and hung up. But when she lifted the receiver, the line was still open.

"Hello."

"Casey? Finally! I thought maybe you'd had a relapse."

She recognized Jeremy's relieved voice immediately.

"No, nothing like that," she assured him. "I was still asleep, and it took me a minute to wake up and get in here."

"How are you feeling today?"

"Much better. My fever hasn't come back and my throat feels almost normal."

"Well, just take it easy today. Are you feeling well enough to fix yourself something to eat?"

"Yes. I think I'll have some tea and scrambled eggs."

"That sounds about right. I wouldn't eat anything too heavy."

"I won't." She paused a moment, and when she spoke it was in a serious tone. "Jeremy, I can't thank you enough for staying with me yesterday. I can't ever remember being that sick, and it was nice to know that someone cared."

"I was glad to help, Casey. I know what it's like to be sick and alone."

There was silence for a moment, and Casey's heart went out to him. Of course he was referring to the time in his life when his fiancée had deserted him. But he didn't know she knew about that, so she could offer no words of comfort.

"Well, I want you to know how much I appreciate it, Jeremy."

"That's okay. I won't keep you any longer. I just wanted to check and make sure you were all right. Get some rest, and I'll be in touch."

She heard the sharp click that signaled a break in the connection, and slowly she replaced the receiver. She remained seated on the couch, lost in thought, for several minutes. Why was he bothering with her? Why was he taking the risk that personal involvement entailed? Was the old Jeremy resurfacing? Was he learning to trust again? She was intrigued—and exhilarated—by the possibility.

A sudden gnawing in the pit of her stomach reminded her that she hadn't eaten for two days, so she prepared the light snack of scrambled eggs and tea that she'd discussed with Jeremy. That required all her energy, though, and she decided to rest again after she ate, falling quickly asleep.

A ringing awakened her shortly after noon, and she rose sleepily, pulled on her robe and headed for the phone. But when she picked it up she heard only the buzz of the dial tone, and she frowned in puzzlement. Surely she hadn't imagined the ringing. Or had she?

A second, more persistent ring brought an embarrassed smile to her face. It was the doorbell! At least she wasn't hearing things! She walked to the door and opened it a crack, leaving the chain in place.

Her eyes widened in surprise when she peered through the thin opening and recognized Jeremy. She quickly closed the door and slid the chain off.

"Hello." She smiled in welcome, her face reflecting her surprise. "I didn't expect to see you today."

"Molly sent this," he explained, holding up a large container. "It's her homemade chicken-rice soup. She says it's guaranteed to cure anything. I promised her I'd drop it off."

"Homemade soup! That sounds wonderful!" she exclaimed, stepping back to let him enter. "Can you stay for a few minutes?"

"Just a few," he said as he shrugged out of his coat. "I told her I'd make sure you ate some of this before I left."

She started to reach for the container, but he moved it out of her reach.

"No, I'll heat it. You sit down and rest. You still look awfully pale," he said with a frown, his eyes on her face.

"Oh, I feel much better, really," she assured him. "That soup is probably just what I need."

"Well, I've had Molly's homemade soup before, and I think you might be right. Go ahead and sit down. This will just take a minute."

Casey did as directed, seating herself in a chair that afforded her a view of the kitchen. She watched him deftly open the container of soup and pour a generous portion into the pot. As, intent on his task, he stirred the soup, she had the chance to study him unobserved.

He had a flair for choosing clothes that enhanced his natural good looks. Yet he seemed unaware of his attractiveness. Perhaps that was what made it so appealing, Casey mused. But in any case, she definitely approved of his apparel today. His beige slacks, off-white shirt with the sleeves rolled up to just below the elbows, and argyle sweater vest made him look particularly young.

What was it about him that so intrigued her? she wondered again. The answer was elusive. All she knew was that whenever she was in his presence her heart began to behave strangely and she felt unexplainably excited and breathless. It was puzzling.

Suddenly, as if sensing that he was the subject of her thoughts, Jeremy turned and looked at her. Embarrassed, Casey lowered her eyes and searched frantically for something to say.

''I . . . I must look a sight,'' she said, voicing the first thing that came to mind. ''While you do that, I'm going to freshen up a bit.''

''You look fine to me.''

''Then I think you need to have your eyes examined,'' she said, flashing him a grin as she left the room.

A few minutes later, after brushing her hair, washing her face, and putting on some lipstick, she returned to the living room. Jeremy was waiting for her, and he rose as she entered.

"That is an improvement," he admitted, the ghost of a smile flickering across his face.

"I don't know if it's *much* of an improvement," she said in chagrin, "but at least I feel better."

"Here's the soup. I can't leave until you start eating it. I promised Molly."

"What about your lunch?" she asked in surprise.

"I'll grab a bite on the way back to the office."

Disappointment welled up inside her, but she struggled to hide it with a smile. Of course he had to get back. He'd been out of the office all afternoon yesterday because of her. She couldn't expect him to stay today. But she wished he could. There was something comforting about his presence.

"Mmm, this is delicious," she proclaimed after her first spoonful of soup. "Please tell Molly how much I appreciate it."

"I will." He rose, restraining her with a hand. "Don't get up. I can find my way out." He retrieved his coat from the closet. "I'll call tomorrow to see how you're doing."

After he left, Casey finished her soup, washed the dishes, and then decided to continue reading a novel she'd started before the Colorado trip. That occupied her most of the afternoon. After cooking a simple dinner and taking a shower, she found that she was exhausted, and she went to bed early.

As promised, Jeremy called the next day about noon, just as Casey was finishing the last of Molly's soup.

"How's the patient today?" he inquired.

"Much better," she replied honestly. "In fact, I feel guilty about staying home."

"You need the rest."

"Maybe," she said, not convinced. "But I'll be in tomorrow."

"No need to rush. Don't come back until you feel back to normal."

"I do. I really don't want to spend another day in this apartment. Besides, I want to see the slides from Colorado."

"They should be in tomorrow. But they can wait, Casey. Don't push yourself."

"I'm not. I really want to come back tomorrow."

True to her word, the next morning she was at the office even earlier than usual. She heard Jeremy enter soon after she arrived, and a moment later he stuck his head in her office. "So. You made it. How do you feel?"

"Fine. Eager to get back to work."

"You do look better," he said analytically, tilting his head to one side and folding his arms. "Molly's soup must have done the trick."

"That, plus some very powerful medicine—and TLC," she added, smiling up at him.

"Just call me Dr. Morgan," he replied with a grin. "By the way, the slides are here."

They spent the next hour or two examining the results of their work in Breckenridge. Jeremy made a few comments here and there, critiquing one slide, complimenting another. Casey learned a great deal during their evaluation session, and she told him so.

"No one ever stops learning. Or they shouldn't," he said. "But you've got all the basics down. That was a fine first assignment. I think you're ready to solo."

Casey's heart took a sudden, sickening dive. She was glad, of course, that he was pleased with her work, but disappointed that they would not be covering another assignment together.

As Christmas approached, Casey saw very little of Jeremy. He was out on assignment about half of the time, and when he was in town he was involved in meetings or working with the magazine's designers.

She sat in on many of these meetings, and although Jeremy was considerate and patiently explained unfamiliar procedures, she sensed that the special warmth that had grown between them during the Colorado trip had evaporated. He was as he had been when she first started at the magazine—polite, businesslike, and impersonal.

She had almost decided not to make good on her promise to have him over for dinner when the perfect opportunity to issue such an invitation presented itself. They had just finished going over some final layouts for the Breckenridge story, working later than usual. As they put on their coats and prepared to leave, Jeremy volunteered to accompany her to her car.

"That's all right," she protested, not wishing to put him to any trouble.

"I'd feel better about it," he said. "The parking lot is probably deserted."

She gave in, and as they descended in the elevator she took a deep breath, realizing that she would never have a better opportunity to ask him to dinner. And she *had* promised.

"Remember when I was sick and you missed dinner, and I said I'd invite you to dinner sometime to make up for that?" she asked a bit breathlessly. "Well, I was wondering if you'd like to come next Saturday."

She didn't dare look up at him, but she held her breath as she waited for his response.

"That's really not necessary, Casey," he said at last. "You don't owe me anything."

"I'd still like to do it. Besides, it will give me a chance to fix a nice meal. I like to cook, but I usually don't bother just for myself. Of course, if you're busy that night, it's all right," she added quickly, not wanting him to feel obligated to accept her hospitality.

"No, I'm free." There was another pause, as if he was carefully considering the invitation. At last he spoke. "I'd like to come. I just don't want you to feel that you owe me anything."

"Well, Christmas is next week. So let's just say we're celebrating the holidays," she replied, her heart soaring. He'd accepted! Maybe, just maybe, they could reestablish the easy camaraderie they'd had on the Breckenridge trip. This would be the perfect opportunity.

Casey spent the next few days decorating her apartment for Christmas. She set out candles and Christmas figurines and even bought a small fir tree to decorate.

Then she planned the menu for Saturday. She would start off with rich, creamy cheese soup, her mother's secret recipe. Next she would serve chicken cordon bleu, a savory potato-and-cheese casserole, green beans almondine, and homemade Sally Lunn bread. For dessert she would prepare one of her specialties, a fudge-almond torte, dense with ground almonds and incredibly rich. There could be no complaints about that menu!

Casey prepared the dessert Friday night, and also did the preliminary preparations for the entrée. Saturday she continued her preparations, doing as much in advance as possible. Finally, when everything was in readiness, she left the kitchen to dress.

She chose her outfit carefully, slipping on a taupe dress, with long, full sleeves and a white lace collar. The dress flowed gracefully when she moved, and its wide burgundy cumberbund emphasized her tiny waist. Then she touched up her makeup and added a drop of her favorite perfume.

She had just finished lighting the candles in the living room and putting the potatoes in the oven when the doorbell rang.

She took a deep breath to steady her pounding heart, telling herself that she was making much more out of this evening than was wise. After all, it was simply the repayment of a debt. But if that was the case, why did she feel so shaky inside?

Her cheeks still flushed from the oven, Casey opened the door to admit Jeremy, determined to be as casual about this evening as she was sure he would be.

"Hi, Jeremy. Come in."

"Hello, Casey. You look lovely tonight. And your apartment looks very Christmasy." He shrugged out of his coat, and Casey sensed a stiff, formal politeness in his manner that did not bode well for a relaxing evening. Her heart fell, but she was determined to be as cheerful as possible.

"Thanks. I love Christmas. Even though I'll be spending it with my family, I couldn't resist a little decorating," she replied as she turned away to hang up his coat.

"This is for you," he said, handing her a small box when she faced him once more. She looked up at him in surprise.

"What is it?"

"It's not much, but I thought of you when I saw it."

She fumbled with the paper as she opened the box, pushing the tissue aside to reveal a Christmas ornament of a tiny skier. In his scrawling hand, Jeremy had written on the enclosed card, *A souvenir of your first assignment. Merry Christmas.*

"Why, Jeremy, thank you," she said, touched by his thoughtfulness. "I'll put it on the tree right now."

After she had done so, she brought them each a glass of eggnog and they sat on the couch, sipping the rich beverage in the flickering candlelight as Christmas carols played in the background.

"This is very nice," Jeremy said softly. "You've managed to create a perfect Christmas mood."

"Thank you." A pleased flush rose on her cheeks. "I hope you brought an appetite tonight."

"Of course. It's not often that I'm treated to a home-cooked meal. So I've been saving up my calories."

"Let's eat, then."

Casey had set the table carefully with a white lace tablecloth over a solid red cloth. Red candles burned in silver candlesticks, their flames reflecting in her sparkling white china. She had made the centerpiece herself, of pinecones, holly, and greenery.

Jeremy gazed at the table for a long moment, and when he turned to her she saw a new warmth in his eyes.

"You've gone to a great deal of trouble, Casey. You didn't have to, you know."

"I wanted to. I like to do nice things for my friends."

She had taken a chance, putting their relationship on more than a coworker level, and she held her breath, wondering how he would respond, or if he would even notice. But she had underestimated Jeremy's perceptiveness.

"Do you consider me a friend?" he asked quietly, a faint echo of surprise in his voice. His intense eyes were riveted on hers, as if her answer was very important.

"Yes, I do." She met his gaze squarely. She wanted to ask him if he considered her a friend, but she didn't dare. She hoped he would volunteer the information, but when he didn't, she forced herself to smile. "I'll serve the soup now. I hope you like it. It's an old family recipe."

It was apparent that Jeremy liked not only the soup, but also everything else she had prepared. He had two helpings of the potato casserole and green beans, and two pieces of the chocolate torte. As they ate, he seemed to grow more and more relaxed, and soon they were chatting as they had the night they dined at the Victorian restaurant in Colorado.

They lingered long over dinner, finally moving back into the living room after she declined his offer to help wash the dishes. Casey lost track of time as they talked. So did Jeremy, apparently, for when he did check his watch, his eyes widened in surprise.

"I had no idea it was this late!" he exclaimed. "Do you realize it's nearly one?"

"I can't believe it!" she replied, honestly surprised. It seemed as if they'd been talking for only a few minutes.

"I should be going," he said, but Casey heard the reluctance in his voice. "You probably have to get up early tomorrow."

"I do have some errands to run and this is my last chance to shop before I go home for Christmas," she admitted. "But you don't have to leave yet." She didn't want him to go. She didn't want this night to end.

"Yes, I do. I've kept you up late enough." He spoke firmly, but with regret. "You're still recovering and you need your rest." He rose, and she followed him to the door, removing his coat from the hall closet.

As Casey watched him slip his arms into it and wrap a wool scarf around his neck, she suddenly realized how dear he had become to her in only a month. She admired the way he had come to terms with his disability. He continued to excel at a physically demanding job, to stay in superb shape, and he never used his disability as an excuse.

At the same time, while he seemed to have made a remarkable physical recovery, she knew that the emotional scars from his fiancée's rejection ran deep. In the long run, that particular hurt, though less visible, had had the most lasting impact. If only she could ease some of his hurt, show him that not all women were like his fiancée, make him realize that to her his physical impairment was irrelevant.

As these thoughts raced through her mind, her fingers played absently with the thin gold necklace she wore. Suddenly Jeremy reached over and took her hand, stilling its nervous movement.

"Is everything all right, Casey?" he asked softly, his eyes locked on to hers.

No, she wanted to say. *I've never felt this kind of longing before. I care about you so much, but I don't know how to reach you. Help me.*

"Yes," she replied instead.

But he read something different in her eyes. Hesitantly, he reached over and touched her face. She held her breath, willing him to take her in his arms. Suddenly, as if reading her mind, he pulled her close and held her with a fierceness that seemed born of desperation, that spoke of a yearning long held in check. She felt a shuddering sigh run through him.

For a long time he just held her, without speaking. Then gently, very gently, he pushed her hair aside and let his lips travel lightly across her neck, leaving a trail of fire in their wake. At last they came down on her lips in a brief kiss as light as a drifting leaf.

Finally he pulled back, his troubled eyes searching

hers. "I didn't want this to happen," he said, almost to himself. "What is it about you that makes all my resolutions crumble?"

Casey stared at him mutely as he ran a fingertip tenderly down the side of her face.

"I have to go," he said, his voice uneven, uncertain. "Thank you for a lovely evening. It's one I'll remember for a long time."

The words sounded almost like a farewell, and Casey looked at him in confusion. There was a wistful sadness in his eyes that caught at her heart with a painful wrench.

He opened the door and stepped into the hall. She followed him, leaning against the doorframe. At the top of the stairs he turned and raised his hand. "Good night, Casey. It's been a wonderful evening."

"It has been for me too." Could he read in her eyes just how wonderful?

But if he could, he made no comment. Instead, with one more wave, he turned and was gone.

She watched him go with a deep, inexplicable ache of sadness. She had the strangest feeling that, in some way, his last comment had been a good-bye, an ending to something. But to what? Nothing had ever really begun.

Worst of all, she had a terrible feeling that whatever Jeremy had decided about their relationship, there was absolutely nothing she could do to change his mind.

Chapter Seven

Casey's intuition proved to be correct. Monday morning, Jeremy thanked her politely for the dinner, and though his manner was warm, it was a friendly warmth—the kind one coworker would have for another.

Certainly he was pleasant. But pleasant was no longer enough for Casey now that she was rapidly losing her heart to him.

Logic told her that it was too soon to be in love. And maybe she wasn't. But with the slightest encouragement she knew that she could be.

Jeremy filled so many of her waking thoughts that even her family noticed her distraction when she went home for Christmas. They were decorating the tree on Christmas Eve when her brother suddenly started laughing.

"Boy, I think she's got it bad," he teased, his eyes twinkling.

It took a moment for his comment to penetrate her consciousness, and when it did she looked over at him.

"What are you talking about?" she asked with a frown.

"Well, I didn't think it was customary to put all the tinsel in one place. Or is that the latest fashion in Chicago?"

Casey looked at the tree and realized that she had been absently piling tinsel on one branch. The fragrant green bough was no longer even visible. Coloring deeply, she began to remove some of the silver strands.

"My mind was on something else," she said non-committally, hoping Rob would drop the subject. But he had other ideas.

"Well, who is he?" he persisted good-naturedly.

"Who's who?"

"This guy you've fallen for."

"Come off it, Rob! Just because I'm a little absentminded today doesn't mean I'm thinking about a man. There are other subjects that occupy a woman's thoughts."

"True. Like world events, the state of the economy, that sort of thing?" he offered helpfully.

"Right."

"So who is he?" he asked again with a grin.

"Rob, I think we ought to change the subject," Casey's mother said. "I'm sure if Casey has anything to tell us she'll do it in her own time."

Casey gave her mother a grateful look, and the older woman smiled understandingly in return.

"Okay," Rob relented with a sheepish grin. "Sorry, Casey. I didn't mean to be nosy."

"It's okay, Rob. There's really nothing to tell or you all would be the first to know." Her eyes clouded momentarily. If only there were something to tell!

"Casey, will you hand me the star for the top of the tree?" her father asked from his perch on the ladder, and she eagerly complied, glad to put her mind on something else.

Later that evening, as the two women baked a last-minute batch of Christmas cookies, her mother cast an anxious eye in Casey's direction.

"Casey dear, you know I'd never pry. I know you're quite capable of handling your life without a lot of advice. But I have noticed that you've seemed rather preoccupied all day, and if there's anything you want to talk about I'll be glad to listen."

Casey looked at the tall, slender woman standing next to the stove, and a surge of affection rushed through her. She had missed their heart-to-heart talks more than she'd realized.

With a sudden pang she also became aware that time was passing. Her mother's clear, understanding eyes were the same, but signs of age were beginning to appear. There were fine lines at the corners of her eyes, and her thick, soft hair, once a deep chestnut brown, was slightly faded and streaked with gray. She still wore it long, though, braided into a chic chignon, because her father liked it that way.

Seeing her parents together, Casey knew she was seeing love as it should be. Theirs was a love that had grown through the years. They had never taken each other for granted, and perhaps that was part of their secret. They worked at their marriage, worked to keep it fresh and new, and, as a result, they never seemed at a loss for something to talk about, as many couples did. They still enjoyed sharing their thoughts and activities.

Her mother took pains to stay in shape and to dress nicely, and her father, in turn, never forgot to show— with a hug, or a kiss, or just a touch—how special she was to him. Theirs was a model marriage, and Casey fervently hoped that someday she would be blessed with one equally wonderful and satisfying.

With a sudden rush of tenderness, she impulsively hugged her mother.

"Oh, Mom, I do need to talk. I'm so mixed up right now. And Rob was right," she admitted with a sigh. "There is a man at the heart of it."

"I thought as much," her mother said. "Sit down and I'll make some tea while we talk."

So as they sipped tea in the kitchen, seated at the familiar oak table of her childhood, Casey poured out the story, haltingly at first, and then more and more quickly. She spoke of her new job and her life in Chicago, but mostly she talked about Jeremy.

Amanda Randall listened quietly, in that special way she had of letting Casey know that for this moment she was the only thing in the world that mattered. When Casey finished, Amanda reached across the table and took her hand.

"You care for him very much, don't you, dear? I can see it in your eyes," she said gently.

"Yes, I do," Casey admitted. "More than I would have thought possible in this short amount of time. Mom, I think I'm falling in love with him. But he doesn't feel the same way about me, and I don't know what to do about it." Her voice reflected her despair.

"It sounds as if he's been hurt deeply, Casey. Maybe he's being cautious. Maybe he just needs time."

"But waiting is so hard! To work that closely with him, feeling as I do . . . ." Her voice trailed off.

"I know, honey. I wish I could offer you some better advice."

Casey looked at Amanda and smiled. "Just listening has been a great help, Mom. I haven't been able to talk with anyone about this, and I do feel better now."

"Those cookies smell great!" Rob exclaimed, bursting through the door in his usual energetic manner. "Are you giving free samples?"

His entrance broke the serious mood, and with a final squeeze of her mother's hand, Casey smiled and stood up.

"One of the first things you'll learn in the business world is that there's no such thing as a free lunch, young man," she said with mock sternness. "You'll have to work for it." She gestured toward the mixing bowls and cookie pans piled in the sink.

"It figures," he said with a groan. "There are always strings attached." Then, with a quick grin, he rolled up his sleeves. "Okay. I'll wash. But I hope those cookies are worth it."

"There's only one way to find out," she said with a laugh, and then turned toward Amanda. "Mom, why don't you go in by the tree and rest awhile? We'll handle things in here."

"Thank you, dear. I'll do that," Amanda said, removing her apron. "Your father is probably lonesome all by himself in there," she added with a wink.

As they tidied up the kitchen, Rob and Casey chatted companionably, catching up on each other's news. He told her about college and his plans for law school, and she spoke about her job and working for Jeremy.

"So he's the one," Rob said quietly.

Casey looked over and met her brother's understanding eyes, and with a jolt she realized that he wasn't her "little" brother anymore. He was a grown man, and a sensitive one at that. When had that transformation occurred?

"Yes, he's the one," she admitted finally, turning away to put a bowl back in its place.

"I'd like to meet him sometime. If you feel that way about him, he must be someone special."

"Why don't you come up for the weekend during spring break?" Casey asked with sudden inspiration.

His eyes lit up. "Seriously? That would be great! I haven't been to Chicago in years."

"Let's plan on it, then."

The Christmas holidays passed all too swiftly, but Casey returned to Chicago feeling renewed and strengthened by her contact with her family.

Jeremy, too, had gone home for Christmas, and he returned seemingly committed to following the pattern he had established for their relationship before the holidays—warm and friendly, but nothing too personal.

Casey actually saw very little of him during the remainder of the winter. Both she and he were traveling a great deal—usually in opposite directions—and when one was in town, the other was frequently on the road.

Occasionally, when they were both in Chicago at the same time, they had lunch together. Although Casey savored those times and held the memory of them in her heart, she also dreaded them. For each time she was with Jeremy she found it harder to accept being "just pals." In many ways it had been easier to cope with the no-nonsense, businesslike attitude he'd exhibited when she'd first started the job.

As the weeks went by, Casey felt her natural optimism slowly fading, and she looked forward more eagerly than she'd expected to Rob's visit. Just being in his buoyant presence would raise her spirits.

He arrived early, suddenly appearing in her office one Friday at noon. She looked up to see who was standing in the doorway, and a delighted smile spread across her face.

"Rob! What are you doing here? I didn't expect you till tonight."

"I couldn't wait to see my favorite sister," he said with a grin. "Besides, I wanted to have a chance to visit your office. And I thought I'd treat you to lunch."

"You're on! Oh, it's good to see you!" she said, moving swiftly around her desk. She was quickly engulfed in a hearty hug.

"Sorry if I'm interrupting anything."

Jeremy's reserved voice interrupted their embrace, and Casey turned to him. He was standing in the doorway between his office and hers, his arms folded across his chest, and his eyes were wary.

"Jeremy!" Her voice faltered, but she quickly regained her composure. "I'd like you to meet my brother, Rob. Rob, Jeremy Morgan."

Suddenly Jeremy's eyes lost their guarded look, and he smiled.

''Nice to meet you, Rob,'' he said warmly, extending his hand. ''Welcome to Chicago.''

''Thanks,'' Rob replied, returning the older man's firm handshake. They had sized each other up quickly and apparently liked what they saw. ''I was just trying to steal Casey away for lunch.''

''Do you mind if I join you? Or would I be intruding on a family reunion?''

Casey looked at him in surprise, but Rob responded before she had a chance to recover.

''Of course not. Casey and I have all weekend to visit. That's okay with you, isn't it, Casey?''

''Sure.'' Somehow she felt as if she'd lost control of the situation. Why did Jeremy want to have lunch with them? What would the three of them talk about? And was this tactful, self-assured man actually her ''little'' brother?

Despite her misgivings, lunch was very pleasant. Rob and Jeremy found plenty to talk about, and Casey was content to sit back and observe the two men. They chatted about a variety of topics, from sports to politics, and Casey felt a glow of pride as Rob held his own throughout the conversation, offering thoughtful opinions. By the time lunch ended, the two men seemed like old friends.

As they rose to leave, Rob and Jeremy shook hands warmly.

''It was a pleasure meeting you, Rob,'' Jeremy said with a smile.

"Thank you. I enjoyed the lunch."

"Casey, why don't you take the rest of the afternoon off?" Jeremy suggested. "Rob's visit will be short, so you might as well take advantage of every minute."

"Oh, I couldn't," she said quickly. "It wouldn't be right."

"Of course it would. You put in plenty of extra hours when you're on the road. Just consider it comp time."

"Come on, Casey," Rob cajoled. "If the boss says it's okay. . . ."

Casey looked from one to the other uncertainly. She'd never played hooky before, and her conscience told her not to now. But Jeremy's argument was persuasive. She did work long hours on the road. And she would like to have more time with Rob.

"Okay," she capitulated at last with a smile. "You win. I can't argue with both of you. Thanks, Jeremy."

"My pleasure." With a wave, he left them outside the restaurant. They watched in silence as he walked away.

"It's really a shame about that limp," Rob observed. "Why do things like that always have to happen to the good people?"

"What?" Casey said abstractedly. "Oh, his limp. I never even notice it anymore," she added truthfully.

"I can see why you like him. He's a great guy. Any chance that something might develop?"

" 'Fraid not, pal.'' She forced her stiff lips to curve upward. "I'm simply a friend and coworker. I don't think romance is among Jeremy's priorities."

"I'm sorry, Casey," Rob said, giving her shoulder a gentle squeeze.

"So am I," she admitted. "But let's not dwell on unpleasant things this weekend. I want us to have fun."

And they did. A stage show, a concert, the museum, shopping, a baseball game, and dining out kept them on the run. By the time Casey waved him off Monday morning and arrived at the office, she was exhausted. She sank into her chair and closed her eyes, mentally trying to prepare herself for the day ahead.

"Looks like you had a rough weekend," Jeremy observed from the doorway. "If I didn't know better, I'd say you'd been to a couple of wild parties."

She looked up to find him lounging against the doorframe, his hands in his pockets, a smile on his face. Even dressed casually, with his shirt sleeves rolled up, he exuded a raw masculinity that stirred her senses. It was getting harder and harder to maintain a "just friends" impersonal tone in his presence.

" 'Whirlwind' would be a more appropriate way to describe the past forty-eight hours," she replied, rolling her eyes. "I must be getting old. Rob was fresh as a daisy when he left this morning."

"Yes, I can see that a woman of your advanced years would find a weekend with Rob tiring," he teased.

She made a face at him, enjoying the repartee. "Ha, ha. But you ought to try to keep up with him. If the government is ever looking for another alternative energy source, I think Rob might qualify."

"He's a great guy," Jeremy said. "I can see why you two get along so well."

"We've always been close, more so than most brothers and sisters. We never fought like kids usually do. I just wish we could see each other more often. I guess I realized for the first time at Christmas how fast things are changing. He'll be even farther away next year when he's in law school."

"There's always the telephone."

"True. But it's not the same. However, speaking of phones, I've got a couple of calls I need to discuss with you," she said, moving the conversation back to a business level.

The pattern of her life continued without much variation as the days passed. Jeremy wasn't in the office much during the next month, and when Casey finally did see him it was in a most unexpected place. She had decided to take a walk and enjoy the early-spring weather one sunny Saturday. She even stopped to chat with a woman working in a tiny garden, admiring the lilac bush laden with blossoms. Before she could protest, the woman had snipped off several large sprays and placed them in Casey's arms.

"Enjoy them," she said, waving Casey's thanks aside. "It does my heart good to find someone who appreciates them. Most people don't even notice flowers anymore. Too busy with 'important' things," the woman said in disgust.

It wasn't until she was halfway home that the sun went in, the wind picked up, and the temperature plunged. Casey increased her pace, berating herself for not wearing a warmer jacket. She knew how unpredictable the weather was at this time of year.

Suddenly a honking horn startled her. With a frown she stopped and turned in the direction of the noise. Jeremy's car pulled up at the curb, and he leaned across to the passenger's side and rolled down the window.

"I thought it was you behind all those flowers," he said with a grin. "Can I give you a lift? The weather's turning pretty nasty."

"Thanks," Casey said a bit breathlessly. He always had that effect on her, and his unexpected appearance quickened her pulse and heightened her color more than usual. He pushed the door open and she got in, carefully settling the flowers in her lap.

"Pretty," he commented, touching one lightly. "Where did you get them?"

"I stopped to admire them, and the woman who owned the garden gave me a bouquet." She lifted one graceful spray and sniffed it. "Mmm. I just love the fragrance of lilacs. I always have. There's something about it that holds the promise of new life, that makes me think of new beginnings. When I smell them I always feel optimistic. Even if the day is damp and cold, they remind me that spring isn't far away."

"That's a nice thought," Jeremy said softly. There was a momentary pause, and she felt as if he was suddenly far away. His next words confirmed her suspicion. "The fragrance of lilacs always makes me think of home," he said. "There was a big lilac bush next to our front porch, and in the spring the whole house smelled like lilacs. I've always associated that fragrance with coming home."

"We have a lilac bush in our backyard, next to our summerhouse," Casey volunteered, pleased that he'd shared his memories with her. "It was always one of my favorite spots on a warm evening."

They continued to chat, and all too soon he pulled up to her apartment house.

"Door service, no less," he said with a smile.

"Thank you, Jeremy. I didn't realize the weather would turn nasty so quickly or I wouldn't have wandered so far unprepared. Sorry to take you out of your way. I've probably made you late for something."

He glanced at his watch. "I have a few minutes to spare."

She looked at him, her arms full of lilacs, her heart filled with longing. Why couldn't he care about her the way she had come to care about him? Why couldn't he learn to take a chance on love again? *Trust me,* her eyes pleaded. *I promise never to hurt you.*

Casey was so deep in thought as she searched Jeremy's eyes that it took her a moment to realize that he was looking at her just as intently. His eyes seemed to reflect an inner struggle, and she yearned to know what he was thinking. He made no move to open the door, and she remained quietly seated.

For several long moments they stared at each other. The lavender blue of the lilacs was almost a perfect match for Casey's wide-set, thickly lashed eyes. Her pale-blue, whisper-soft angora sweater softly suggested the gentle curves of her body.

Slowly Jeremy reached over, and with the back of his hand, gently stroked her cheek. She drew in her breath sharply at his touch, and her heart thudded heavily in her chest.

"You're very lovely, Casey," he said softly, his voice a bit hoarse.

She didn't know how to respond, except to stare at him, her eyes wide. The fragrance of lilacs wafted up to her, and she knew that for the rest of her life she would associate lilacs with this moment.

With one more gentle touch, Jeremy withdrew his hand. He started to speak, then stopped and stared out the window. She remained unmoving, and at last he turned back to her.

"I've thought about this for a long time, Casey," he said, taking a deep breath. "I'd like to get to know you better—away from work. I don't know if that's wise. They say business and pleasure don't mix. But they—whoever 'they' are—also say that rules were made to be broken. What do you think?"

"I'd like to give it a try," she replied quietly, her heart singing.

He turned to her, his eyes even more intensely blue than usual as he searched her face. Then he glanced at his watch with a frown.

"I'd like to stay longer now, but I have an appointment. Can we talk more next week?"

She nodded.

He came around and opened the door for her, helping her out of the car with a gentle touch that made her tremble. Then, with one more tender look, he was gone.

Casey watched the car disappear in the distance, and though the chilly wind whipped around her, she was protected by a warm glow of happiness.

Chapter Eight

When Casey entered her office on Monday morning, her spirits were high. A delicious tingle of excitement ran through her as she considered the promise of Jeremy's parting words. It seemed he was at last willing to take the risk of a relationship again.

She peeked into Jeremy's office when she arrived, but it was still dark. That was odd. Usually he arrived earlier than she did. Perhaps he had been delayed in traffic.

Casey forced herself to tackle the correspondence on her desk, but her mind was not really on her work. She listened with mounting anticipation for the sound of Jeremy's door being opened.

As the minutes dragged by and he did not appear, she grew worried. It wasn't like him to be late.

A sudden sound made her jump, and the pen that she held in her hand drew a squiggly line on the paper.

She really was on edge! She looked up and saw Molly standing there.

" 'Morning Casey,'' Molly said, smiling. "I don't want to disturb you, but I wanted to let you know that Jeremy won't be in today.''

"Oh?'' A wave of disappointment swept over Casey and her heart sank. Molly looked at her crest-fallen face in surprise.

"Is something wrong?'' she asked in concern. "We can probably reach him if it's an emergency.''

"No, no,'' Casey said quickly, struggling to compose her face. "I'm just surprised. Is he sick?''

"No. He had to reshoot something for the New England story. I guess he was in here Saturday to look at the film he shot last week, and he apparently wasn't happy with it. He left a note on my desk saying he'd be back later in the week. Do you need to talk with him if he calls?''

"No.''

"Okay.'' With a last speculative look, Molly left.

Casey forced herself to examine the situation logically. It wasn't as if Jeremy was avoiding her. Something had simply come up that required his attention, causing a temporary delay. That thought comforted her, and she was able to tackle her work with a clearer mind.

As the week progressed, however, her sense of anticipation and excitement again began to grow. When she finally heard his door open on Thursday afternoon, she felt like a schoolgirl about to meet her first date.

When Jeremy entered her office a few moments later, his deep blue eyes smiled warmly into hers, and Casey discovered that she was actually trembling. Did he have any idea what a devastating effect he had on her emotions? She doubted it. He seemed totally at ease, completely unaware of how attractive he was.

Casey carefully set down the glass of water she was holding, afraid that he would notice how badly her hand was shaking. The intensity of her attraction to him was almost frightening. Although she'd dated quite a bit, no one had ever had this effect on her, even though several of the men had obviously had romantic intentions. Jeremy, on the other hand, had given her virtually no encouragement. Yet the strength of her response to him was almost overwhelming.

Perhaps it was simply a physical attraction, she mused. But she really didn't believe that. At first, although she'd thought him attractive, she hadn't been drawn to him in this way. But as she'd grown to know him, she had come to admire, respect—and, yes, love him, she could now admit. And along with that love she had found herself becoming more and more attracted to him on a purely physical level as well. The problem was how to control her feelings. She didn't want to rush Jeremy into something he was not yet ready to face.

"Welcome back," she said, forcing her trembling lips into a smile.

"Thanks. Talk about an unexpected trip! I knew when I was shooting last week that the weather wasn't ideal. I just crossed my fingers and hoped the shots would come out. But when I stopped by here to check them Saturday, after I dropped you off, I knew I had to reshoot. I came back as quickly as I could, though."

He strolled over and perched on her desk, and her heart went into a staccato beat at his nearness.

"I missed you, Casey," he said softly, and his eyes held a new tenderness that touched her heart.

"I missed you too," she admitted, her voice tight with emotion. Could this really be happening? She had all but given up any hope of ever winning Jeremy's heart.

"I know it's awfully late to ask you for this weekend, but Sunday is supposed to be a beautiful day. Is there any chance you're free? A friend of mine has a farm, and we could go up for the day, maybe do a little riding."

"Sunday would be fine," she agreed. A whole day in Jeremy's company! Could anything be more perfect?

He rose and smiled down at her. "I'll be looking forward to it."

"So will I."

Friday and Saturday passed in a haze of happiness.

Casey felt as if her feet had wings, and she fairly floated through the days. Saturday night she found sleep elusive and dozed on and off. She berated herself for being such a romantic fool, but she couldn't help it. Everything seemed to be going so perfectly that she resented having to give up this feeling of euphoric happiness for even a few hours while she slept.

Although she didn't get much rest, excitement added a sparkle to her eyes and brought a flush to her cheeks on Sunday, and she looked as fresh as if she'd slept for eight hours. She dressed casually, as Jeremy had suggested, in jeans, a cotton shirt and a long-sleeved sweater. She also took along a windbreaker, but the day was sunny and warm already, and she doubted whether she would need it.

Jeremy arrived promptly at eight-thirty, and as she opened the door to admit him she once again found herself a bit breathless in his presence. He was dressed in jeans and an open-necked golf shirt that hugged his broad chest.

''All set to try a bit of horseback riding?'' he asked.

''Yes. I can't wait! I hope these clothes are okay. I haven't done much riding,'' she said doubtfully.

''You look fine,'' he assured her, giving her a brief but approving scrutiny. ''Shall we go?''

They chatted amiably during the two-hour drive, and once they were away from the concrete and noise of Chicago, Casey leaned back and breathed a contented sigh.

"I like the country," she confessed as she eyed the newly green fields and rolling hills around her. "There's something so restful about it."

Jeremy nodded. "I know what you mean. I don't get up to the farm very often, but when I do I always come back with a different, fresher perspective. I think you'll like the place."

At last they turned through the gates leading to the farm, and Casey gazed in delight at the old white, rambling farmhouse. A long veranda traveled around three sides of the two-story structure, and a porch swing and wicker chairs were invitingly placed on the wooden floor.

"Jeremy, this is wonderful! It's like something from a book! Does someone really live here, or is this a stage set?"

Her question was answered when the front door swung open and two little boys and a huge dog spilled out. They were followed by a thirtyish man with a pleasant smile, sandy hair, and a sprinkling of freckles across his nose.

As Jeremy got out of the car, the children catapulted down the steps and threw themselves at him. He swung one of them up in each arm, and they giggled delightedly.

"Hello there! And how are you, Sam?" he asked, reaching down to give the dog a quick pat.

"Hi, Jeremy," the man said as he came down the

steps at a more moderate pace. "Welcome to the nuthouse."

"Hi, Bruce," Jeremy said with a smile. "It's good to see you. And if this is a nuthouse, I'll willingly be committed. You're living most people's fantasy: a wonderful wife, two great kids, a place in the country—what more could you ask?"

"Not much," Bruce admitted with a grin. "It's a perfect setup, and I know it."

"Casey, I'd like you to meet Bruce Weston, an old buddy of mine. Bruce, this is Casey Randall."

"Nice to meet you, Casey. If it's because of you that Jeremy finally decided to visit, then I owe you a debt of gratitude. We haven't seen him in months."

Casey smiled. "I don't think I can claim the credit. But I'm glad he decided to bring me along. You have a wonderful place here."

"We like it. It's about as close to idyllic as you can get." He turned back to Jeremy. "You'd better put the twins down. They may be only six years old, but they're quite an armful."

"They have grown quite a bit," Jeremy conceded. "Mike and Jim, this is Casey. Casey, these are Bruce's pride and joy."

"Hi," she said with a smile.

They smiled shyly, hiding behind Jeremy, who was asking Bruce, "Where's Kathy?"

"She had to go into town today, but she may be back before you leave."

"I hope so. I'd like Casey to meet her. In the meantime, I'm looking forward to a nice ride."

"Well, the horses are waiting for you."

"Great!" Jeremy reached into the backseat of the car and withdrew a large parcel. Noting Casey's curious gaze, he grinned. "Lunch. Riding in the fresh air always makes me hungry."

"I didn't even think about food! I could have fixed something," she said apologetically.

"No, I wanted to do it. Now, on to the barn," he said, closing the subject.

Bruce led the way, and he and Jeremy quickly saddled the two mounts. Jeremy's was a spirited black stallion, and Casey's was a gentle chestnut mare.

"Jeremy said you weren't a very experienced rider, but I hope Scottish Miss won't be too tame for you," Bruce said with a frown.

"Tame is exactly what I'm looking for," Casey assured him. "The gentler the better."

"Then Scottish Miss should be perfect," Bruce said with a relieved smile. He turned to Jeremy, who was stowing the lunch in his saddlebags. "Have a great ride. We'll see you later this afternoon."

With a wave, Bruce and the twins, accompanied by Sam, left the barn.

Jeremy turned to Casey with a smile, apparently sensing her trepidation. "You're not nervous, are you?"

"No. Well, maybe a little," she admitted with a grin.

"No need to be. Scottish Miss is a well-mannered lady. You won't have any trouble. Now, let me give you a hand up."

Casey placed her foot in the stirrup, and with a boost from Jeremy, she swung up into the saddle. The height of the mount surprised her.

"Wow! I feel a long way up!" she exclaimed. "I'd forgotten how high up you are on a horse. It's been years since I've ridden."

"It will come back to you," Jeremy predicted, and Casey watched with admiration as he swung easily and gracefully up into the saddle. "Ready?"

She nodded, and he led the way out of the barn and around the back to a green field bordered by woods. Daffodils and irises were blooming, and the earth smelled sweet and fresh. Jeremy dropped back beside her once they were in the field.

"How are you doing?" he asked.

"Okay. Isn't this a beautiful day?"

"Sharing it with you is what makes it even more beautiful."

Casey gazed at him, her heart so filled with happiness and longing that she thought it would burst. How she wanted to put her arms around him, to feel his lips on hers. Suddenly, afraid that he would read the longing in her eyes, she turned away.

"Oh, look, a deer!" she said in surprise, pointing

toward the woods, glad to be able to draw attention away from herself.

"Yes. If we're lucky, we'll see a few more before the day is over."

They rode in companionable silence much of the time for the next hour, with Jeremy leading the way. At one point, as they were crossing an open field, he turned to her and asked, "Do you mind if I give Starfire a workout for a few minutes?"

"No, not at all." Casey sensed that he was holding back his mount for her benefit, and she was content to sit still for a few minutes anyway. She watched in admiration as he rode away, moving as one with his horse. He was a superb rider, and she was impressed by his skill.

"That was great!" she told him when he drew up beside her. "You're a wonderful rider."

"I enjoy it," he said with a shrug. "I'm not really that good, but it gives me a great sense of freedom to ride like that. Ready to continue?"

They rode for another half hour, emerging at last from a fairly dense wood into a small glade with a brook. Flat gray boulders were scattered on a carpet of green moss, and a small waterfall cascaded down some rocks.

"Oh, how lovely!" she said in a hushed voice, reluctant to disturb the peace of the spot.

"Yes, it is," he agreed. "Would you like to have lunch here?"

"That would be wonderful."

"Stay up there and I'll come over and help you down," he instructed, swinging out of the saddle. When he was next to her he reached up and placed his hands on her waist, lowering her gently to the ground as she swung her leg over the saddle. His hands remained at her waist once she was on the ground, and she looked at him questioningly, her heart missing a beat when she saw the intensity of his eyes. With obvious effort he at last stepped back and smiled.

"Be careful when you walk. You'll probably be a bit stiff," he warned as he moved to his horse and unstrapped his saddlebag. She immediately missed the warm touch of his hands.

She took a couple of tentative steps and found that he was right.

Casey helped Jeremy spread a plastic sheet on the ground, which they covered with a checkered cloth. She watched in astonishment as he withdrew white zinfandel wine, French bread, cheese, cold roast chicken, fresh fruit, a marinated vegetable salad, and chocolate brownies from the parcel he'd stowed in his saddlebag. When he looked up and saw her expression, he laughed.

"Don't get the wrong idea. I'm afraid I'm no cook. All of the credit for this feast goes to Mama Leone's Deli. She packs a great picnic lunch."

"I'll say! This looks wonderful!"

He withdrew two wineglasses and filled them carefully. Then he raised one. "To friendship," he said.

"To friendship," she echoed, and the clink of their glasses broke the stillness of the glade.

The meal was delicious, and after they'd eaten as much as they could hold they leaned back against one of the gray boulders.

"Oh, I don't think I'll ever be able to get back up on Scottish Miss," Casey said with a groan, her eyes closed. "I'm stuffed! Mama Leone is a marvel!"

"Yes, she is. But you're a wonderful cook too. In fact," he said after a moment's pause, "you're pretty wonderful in a lot of ways."

She opened her eyes and turned to look at him. He was watching her as he rested against the rock, his hands behind his head, one knee drawn up.

"No, I'm not," she said, thinking of her relationship with him. "I make mistakes. Things don't always turn out the way I want them to."

"And how do you want this to turn out, Casey?" he asked, reaching over to stroke her cheek with the back of one hand.

The touch of his fingers sent a tremor through her body, and her breath caught in her throat. She was afraid to move, afraid to break the spell. His question was answered in the silent eloquence of her eyes.

Slowly, gently, he reached for her. She went willingly into his arms, a shudder of joy passing through her. For a few moments he just held her, and it was enough to feel his arms around her, to hear the steady beating of his heart. She let her head rest on his shoulder and gently stroked his back.

"You're a very special person, Casey," he whispered softly, his chin resting on her head. "In fact, you're the most remarkable woman I've ever met. You're assertive and feminine at the same time. And you have such a warm, caring heart."

He pulled back and looked down at her. She returned his gaze, her eyes glowing.

"I've wanted to do this for a long time," he said, and then, whisper soft, his lips came down on hers.

Suddenly all the sweet longing that she had tried so hard to suppress surged up with an intensity that startled her. As his kiss continued, a long, sweet shiver of delight ran through her. He crushed her slight body against his, and she ran her fingers through the hair at the base of his neck, luxuriating in its softness. Time seemed to stop as they clung to each other. She wanted the moment to last forever.

His lips traveled across her neck, pausing in the hollow at the base of her throat, and a sigh of delight escaped her lips. She had never fully understood before when friends talked about the ecstasy of being in a man's arms. Now she had a glimpse of that indescribable joy.

Jeremy's lips were warm and lingering, but at last, with a shaky breath, he drew away. Casey lovingly traced with her eyes the strong outlines of his face.

His tender look melted her heart, and for the first time since she'd met him he seemed totally relaxed, his wariness gone.

"I'd forgotten how this felt," he said, his eyes smiling down into hers.

"I never even knew," she admitted, her eyes glowing.

"Oh, Casey, this has been such a wonderful day," he said with a sigh, pulling her toward him again. She went willingly, snuggling into the warm circle of his arms. She had never before felt such a deep contentment or had such a strong feeling of "rightness." She belonged with Jeremy. If she had ever harbored any doubts, they were now gone.

They sat that way in silence for a long time, content simply to be together. Occasionally Jeremy stroked the back of Casey's hand with one finger or caressed her shoulder where his hand rested. Now and then they spoke in low tones, but neither seemed willing to break the magic spell with words. Both were reluctant to end what had been a perfect day. But at last, as the shadows lengthened, Jeremy stirred.

"We've got to go back. It's getting late," he said in a muffled voice, his lips in her hair. She could hear the regret in his voice.

"I know," she said with a sigh.

He gently extricated himself and started to stand up. As he did so, Casey saw a spasm of pain flash across his face. Instinctively, with a worried frown, she reached out to him. "Jeremy?"

He gave her a wry grin. "Sometimes my leg stiffens up when I've been in the same position too long," he explained. "It will be fine in a minute."

He stood up more carefully and walked back and forth in front of her a couple of times.

"See? Good as new," he said with a smile, reaching down to help her to her feet. In one swift movement she was beside him.

"Are you sure you're all right?" she asked in concern.

"Absolutely."

"Okay." She didn't question him further, not wanting to make an issue of his limp. And he did seem to be fine now. But it was apparent that pain was still part of his life.

They walked hand in hand back to their horses, and stayed close beside each other during the ride back. They took their time, savoring the special closeness that had developed between them, wanting to keep the world at bay as long as possible.

But all too soon they reached the barn. With Bruce's help, Jeremy unsaddled and rubbed down the horses while Casey chatted with Kathy, a young woman who at any other time she would have found delightful. But today her thoughts were on Jeremy, and it took all her willpower to keep her eyes from straying to him as she talked with Bruce's wife.

At last they were in the car and headed back to the city. Jeremy reached for her hand and held it during most of the drive. When they arrived at her apartment, he accompanied her to the door.

"Be sure and take a hot bath right away," he instructed. "Otherwise you'll be sore tomorrow."

"I will." She fitted her key into the lock and turned to him. "Would you like to come in?"

"Yes," he said with a smile. "But I won't. That would be tempting fate."

She looked up at him, and the depth of longing in his eyes made her pulse flutter.

"I can't thank you enough for today, Jeremy," she said a bit breathlessly. "It was the nicest day I can ever remember."

"I feel the same way." He brushed a strand of hair back from her face and then leaned toward her. Though his touch was gentle, she felt as if her lips were burning as they met his.

"Good night, Casey. Sweet dreams." He gave her a hand a gentle squeeze and was gone.

Chapter Nine

Casey awoke the next morning with a warm feeling of well-being. For a moment, in her half-awake state, she could find no explanation for her buoyant happiness. Then, as sleep vanished, she recalled her day with Jeremy and a smile spread across her face.

With a burst of energy she jumped out of bed, only to lean against the wall, a comic look of surprise on her face. Despite Jeremy's hot-tub prescription, there was no doubt in her mind that she had spent hours on horseback the day before. She was more stiff and sore than she would have thought possible.

Gingerly she took a few steps, grimacing with each one. She could hardly walk! Maybe another soak in a hot tub would help.

The warm water did ease the stiffness somewhat. And movement also seemed to help. In fact, by the time she reached the office much of the stiffness was gone. But she was still sore, she noted, as she carefully eased herself into her chair. When she looked up, Jeremy was grinning at her from the doorway.

"You look like you're walking on eggs," he said cheerfully.

She made a face at him. "Let's just say I have a souvenir of our outing. I suppose you aren't sore at all?"

"No," he admitted with a smile.

"Well, you don't have to be so smug about it!" she said accusingly, but the twinkle in her eye took the sting out of her words.

"Smug? Perish the thought! Did you take a hot bath?"

"Yes. And it didn't work, doctor."

"Of course it did. Just think how you'd feel if you hadn't followed my advice."

She shuddered. "No thanks!"

"My latest prescription is to keep moving today. It's hard to get stiff muscles working at first, but that's the best way to limber them up. I wouldn't attempt anything too strenuous, though."

"Don't worry. I wasn't planning to run a marathon."

"I think that's wise." He walked over and perched on her desk, and she found herself trembling at his nearness. She could see that she was going to have a hard time maintaining a professional attitude at the office after yesterday.

But Jeremy seemed to be doing fine. How was he managing to maintain such a friendly but businesslike manner after the affection they'd shared yesterday? The only indication that anything emotional had occurred between them was a new warmth in his eyes that made her want to melt into his arms.

"I'm going to be gone the rest of the week," he was saying, and she forced herself to pay attention. "I've got to do some shooting in Arizona. Are you going to meet with the author of the Alaska piece this week?"

"Yes. Tomorrow," she answered automatically, all too conscious of the nearness of his taut, muscular frame. She watched his lips as he spoke, and she couldn't help wishing that instead of speaking they were locked on hers in a kiss.

Suddenly she realized that he had stopped talking, and with a start she forced her eyes away from his lips and up to his eyes, which looked at her questioningly.

"I have a feeling you're a million miles away, Casey. You seem very distracted this morning," he said, tilting his head to one side quizzically.

You have only yourself to blame, she wanted to say, but instead she smiled and shrugged sheepishly. "Sorry. I must admit my thoughts did wander for a moment. What were you saying?"

"I said I've looked at the article. You remember, the one on Alaska," he teased. "It's well done. But that's a lot of territory for one photographer to cover.'' He paused for a moment. ''I think we should team up on this one.''

Casey's spirits soared and her eyes sparkled. They hadn't traveled together since the Breckenridge trip, and she had been hoping ever since then that there would be another opportunity for a team assignment.

''Okay,'' she said with a nod, trying to match his friendly but impersonal tone. ''I'll have Molly make the arrangements. Do you want to go next week?''

''That would be fine.'' He rose, reaching over to run a finger down her cheek in an intimate, caressing—but fleeting—gesture. Her heart thumped heavily in her chest, and she longed to reach up and take his hand. But she restrained herself. It would be too easy for things to get out of hand, and this wasn't the time or the place.

He seemed to read her thoughts and he smiled gently.

''I know,'' he said nodding understandingly. ''I feel the same way.''

This time she did reach up and briefly take his hand, and for a long moment they looked into each other's eyes. Words weren't even needed.

With an obvious effort, Jeremy rose.

''I'll be in Friday,'' he said. ''We can talk about the trip then.''

''Okay.'' Her throat was strangely constricted. Did

he have any idea what even a simple touch like that from him did to her pulse rate?

"Have a good week," he said with a tender smile. "I'll be thinking of you."

"I'll be thinking of you too," she replied, knowing that she would be thinking of little else.

And she was right. Although she plunged into work, hoping to take her mind off Jeremy, she frequently found her thoughts drifting to him and forcibly had to concentrate on what was happening around her.

On Tuesday morning, even as she prepared to meet with Dan Green, the author of the Alaska article, she couldn't stop thoughts of Jeremy from intruding on her consciousness. A shiver of delight ran through her as she thought about the upcoming trip with him. It would be wonderful to work together again!

Dan Green appeared in her office right on schedule, and she rose to greet him with a smile. He was about thirty-five, muscular, of medium height, with curly brown hair and twinkling green eyes. He had an outgoing, engaging manner, and Casey immediately recognized in him the spirit of an adventurer. He was even dressed like one, wearing khaki trousers, a coarse, cable-knit sweater and hiking boots—attire more suited to the wide-open spaces than to an office in the heart of Chicago.

"I've read your article," Casey told him as they

shook hands. "It's well done. If I weren't going there on assignment to take photos, your article would make me want to go on my own."

"Thanks. It's a great place."

"You know, this is a luxury we don't often have—meeting an author in person. I usually do this sort of thing by phone. I'm glad you were in town."

"Me too. It just happened to work out this way."

"Well, down to business," she said with a smile, pulling a notepad toward her. "Any hints or suggestions about what we should photograph and where we should go?"

They spent the next hour or so discussing the assignment, and when Casey at last put down her pen she nodded in satisfaction.

"That was a great help, Dan. This will make our job much easier."

"Glad to hear it. I wish I could go back again, but there are too many other places to see and mountains to climb first," he said with a grin.

"How long will you be in Chicago?" she asked.

"I leave Friday. Say, Casey, I don't know if you'd be interested, but the friend I'm staying with gave me a couple of tickets to the ballet Thursday night. He's going out of town, so he can't use them. Would you like to go?"

"To the ballet?" Casey asked in surprise. Dan just didn't look like the type who would enjoy the ballet. She could more easily picture him on a spelunking outing or tramping through the woods in search of wild game. Her surprise must have shown in her face, because he laughed.

"I should probably be insulted," he chided her good-naturedly. "Just because I love the outdoors doesn't mean I don't appreciate cultural things too."

"Oh, I didn't mean that!" she exclaimed, turning deep red.

"It's okay," he assured her. "A lot of people make that mistake. So how about it?"

She hesitated. Dan was a pleasant man. And she had traveled enough in the last few months to know how lonely it was to be in a strange town, especially at night, with no one to talk to. He was probably simply looking for some companionship, and she could empathize with that need.

Why not go with him? It would be a pleasant evening, after all. She would love to see the ballet, which featured one of her favorite artists, and it might take her mind off Jeremy. She smiled and nodded her assent. "That sounds like fun."

"Great!" Dan said enthusiastically. "I'll pick you up about seven. Then we'll get something to eat afterward. How does that sound?"

"Fine," she agreed with a smile.

By the time Thursday night arrived, Casey found herself looking forward to the evening more than she'd expected. She'd worked long hours at the office the last two days, and a relaxing evening was just what she needed. Dan would be a pleasant companion, and she knew that she would enjoy the ballet.

She dressed in a clingy jersey dress of deep blue that showed off her figure to perfection. A beaded sweater and evening bag added just the right touch of formality.

As she dressed she found herself speculating on what Dan would wear. For a man who disliked formality, this type of event seemed out of character. Perhaps he would shun convention and arrive in jeans and a sweater. She grinned at the thought. They'd make quite a pair if he did!

Casey had misjudged him, however. When she opened the door in answer to his ring, she hardly recognized him. He was dressed in a superbly cut three-piece gray suit, white shirt, and maroon-and-silver silk tie. Her astonishment must again have been reflected in her eyes, because he threw back his head and laughed. "Surprise again! You thought I'd show up in jeans, didn't you?"

"Of course not," she lied, blushing furiously.

"Yes, you did. But I forgive you. I'd have to forgive anyone who looked as good as you do." He stepped back and let out a low whistle. "Pardon me for staring. But you look fantastic!"

"Thank you," Casey said, pleased at the compliment. "So do you."

"We make quite a dashing couple, if I do say so myself," he said, lifting his chin and brushing an imaginary speck of dust off his lapel. Then he grinned and offered her his arm. "Shall we?"

"Let's," she replied, laughing.

Dan was charming and attentive, and she found him to be a delightful companion. After the ballet he asked where she would like to eat, and she suggested a place she'd heard about that was popular with the after-theater crowd. They even danced a few dances before they decided to call it a night.

"Thanks, Casey. It's been a lot of fun," he said as he walked her to her door.

"I enjoyed it too. And thanks again for all your photo suggestions for the Alaska piece."

"Glad to be of service. Good night." He leaned over and kissed her lightly on the cheek.

"Good night, Dan."

Casey closed the door, slipped the lock into place, and thoughtfully walked toward her room. It was interesting how you could be attracted to one person and not another. Take Dan, for example. He was charming, well traveled, considerate, intelligent—the kind of man most women would easily fall in love with. Yet she was not attracted to him on any level beyond friendship.

Jeremy, on the other hand, held a special place in her heart. He was harder to understand than any man she'd ever met—but then again, she'd never met a man who had gone through such a physical and emotional trauma. His caution and reserve made it difficult to get to know him.

But he'd let his guard down enough for her to realize that he was a kind, sensitive, warm, caring, highly principled man. How many men would risk their own life to save the life of a little boy? How many would take care of a sick coworker, and a new one at that? She recalled the day of their picnic. How many men would have treated her as Jeremy had, with such tenderness and with no attempt to take advantage of a romantic opportunity? He was like no other man she'd ever met.

The mere thought of seeing him tomorrow made her pulse quicken, and she knew as she climbed into bed and turned out the light that it would be a restless night.

Casey did not sleep well, just as she'd predicted. Nevertheless, she awoke feeling refreshed and excited. She dressed with more care than usual, choosing a soft green skirt and an off-white cotton sweater, and she brushed her hair until it shone. Excitement added a blush of color to her cheeks.

Jeremy was already at the office when she arrived, but his door was closed so she decided not to disturb him. He was probably trying to catch up after being gone most of the week. So she conferred with Molly on the Alaska itinerary to make sure that everything was in order.

"You're covering a lot of territory," Molly commented as they glanced over the schedule. "But with two of you working, it shouldn't be so bad."

"Not bad at all," Casey agreed with a smile. *In more ways than one*, she added silently.

She returned to her office, pausing by Jeremy's still-closed door. She was hesitating uncertainly, debating whether to disturb him, when the door was thrown open with a suddenness that startled her.

Jeremy seemed as taken aback by her presence as she was by his sudden appearance.

"Oh!" she said, startled. Then she laughed shakily. "I think you frightened a year off my life."

"Sorry about that," he apologized, a smile flashing briefly across his face.

Casey looked at him in surprise. The caressing warmth that had been in his voice the last time they were together was noticeably lacking. He sounded polite but businesslike. She felt a chill the way one does on a warm spring day when the sun suddenly hides behind a cloud.

"Is something wrong, Jeremy?" she faltered, knowing that something was very wrong.

"Of course not," he said. "Why do you ask?"

"I don't know," she said, shrugging, her eyes confused. "You just seem . . . different."

"I'm a little tired. My flight got in late last night."

For the first time, Casey took a good look at him. He did appear worn and tired. But he also seemed to have aged considerably since she'd last seen him.

There were lines etched in his face that hadn't been there before, and his eyes seemed bleak and disheartened.

''You don't look well,'' she said in concern. ''Are you sure you're not getting sick?''

''No, I'm fine. I guess I'm just getting too old for those late hours. I can't say the same about you, though. You look as radiant as always, despite being up late.''

''What do you mean?'' she asked in confusion, thrown off guard by his unexpected comment.

''I saw you last night at the restaurant when I stopped for a bite to eat,'' he said carelessly, as if it didn't matter. ''You dance very well.''

She frowned. ''You were there? Why didn't you come over and say hello?''

''I didn't want to interrupt.''

''There was nothing to interrupt.''

''Well, you know what they say. Two's company.'' His smile seemed forced.

Was Jeremy jealous? Casey wondered. Was that why he was acting so strange? But there was no reason for jealousy.

''I was with Dan Green—the author of the Alaska story,'' she explained quickly. ''We met earlier in the week, and he was fortunate enough to get tickets for the ballet. I guess he didn't know anyone else in town to ask.''

"Did you have a nice time?" Jeremy asked politely.

"Yes. It was very nice."

They were like strangers discussing the weather. Casey couldn't believe that this was the same man who'd held and kissed her so tenderly last Sunday.

"That's good. You need to take more time for fun, Casey. You work too hard."

Casey looked at him in confusion. He seemed to be encouraging her to go out with other men. So it was obvious that jealousy couldn't account for his behavior.

What was it, then? What had happened to make him so indifferent toward her? Last Sunday he'd made her think that she was special, that he cared about her deeply. His attitude today was inconsistent with the way he had behaved the last time they'd been together. Or had she misjudged the depth of his feelings?

"Do you have time now to discuss the Alaska trip?" he interrupted her thoughts.

"Yes," she said with a nod, forcing herself to concentrate on his words as she turned and led the way to her office. "You'll notice that I've recovered from the horseback riding," she added over her shoulder, with artificial cheerfulness. Maybe if she reminded him of their outing, his manner would warm.

"So I see. You ought to go more often. I think you'd be a very good rider, given some practice," he said instead, in a friendly, conversational tone.

She ought to go more often. Not *we* ought to go more often. The implication was clear. Jeremy was not planning to take her riding again.

Casey felt physically sick. Her world seemed to be crashing around her, and all she could do was stand by and watch helplessly.

They spent the next hour discussing their plans for Alaska, and it took all her willpower to pay attention. Jeremy occasionally made suggestions, and she noted them automatically. On the whole, though, her research and arrangements were as thorough as always.

"Nice job," he said as he rose to leave.

"Thanks."

"Shall I pick you up Sunday about ten?"

"That's not necessary." It was clear that Jeremy wanted to cool things off, and Casey had too much pride to run after any man, even Jeremy.

She didn't look at him as he stood next to her desk, concentrating instead on arranging the papers before her. She was afraid that if he looked into her eyes he would read the despair and desperate longing in them.

"Are you sure?"

"Yes. I can manage."

He didn't press the issue. "All right. I'll meet you at the airport, then. I can handle the equipment."

"Fine."

"See you Sunday," he said, turning away.

For a long time after he left, Casey sat at her desk, staring into space. She was unaware of the passage of time. Her mind sought possible explanations for his change in attitude. Perhaps he had just decided that business and pleasure didn't mix. Or maybe he had decided that Casey wasn't the kind of woman he wanted to become serious about. Or maybe he was having second thoughts about risking another relationship.

In any case, she knew that love couldn't be forced. It was either there or it wasn't. She had hoped that, given a chance, love would grow between them. And he had definitely given her indications that he felt the same way. Or had she read too much into last Sunday? There were so many things she didn't understand about him. So many things she would probably never understand.

Now she pondered her next move. She'd always known, as Jeremy had once said, that there was a danger in becoming emotionally involved with co-workers. They'd taken the risk and it hadn't worked out. How could she work by his side for the next week in Alaska, aware that he didn't care about her, when her own feelings were so strong?

Her spirits sank, leaving a sick feeling in the pit of her stomach. How could a day that had started out on such a high note end in such disaster? This morning the world had held such promise, and she had looked forward with great excitement and anticipation to their trip next week. Now she dreaded it.

The image of his dispassionate eyes appeared in

her mind. Then she pictured those same eyes—full of warmth and tenderness—as they'd looked at her on the farm. Would Jeremy ever look at her that way again?

There were few times in her life when her sunny, optimistic disposition deserted her, but this was one of them. For Casey felt that something infinitely beautiful and rare and precious had been within her grasp, but that it had slipped away. And, worst of all, she didn't think there was anything she could do to retrieve it.

Chapter Ten

Leaden skies and heavy rains didn't help to raise Casey's spirits when she awoke on Saturday. And she felt no better on Sunday.

For a long time she simply lay in bed staring at the ceiling, but at last she forced herself to get up. Listlessly she made herself a cup of tea. Nothing seemed to matter anymore. The glow had gone out of her life, leaving in its place a numbing emptiness. As she moved about the apartment, she didn't even stop to look out her window at the flowers she'd planted in the small yard. Even their bright colors couldn't lift her spirits today.

As the dark smudges under her eyes testified, she hadn't slept well. She tried unsuccessfully to camouflage them with makeup, giving up at last with a sigh. Jeremy wasn't likely to notice anyway.

But she was wrong. Her appearance was the first thing he commented on when they met at the airport.

"You look tired," he said with a frown. "Are you feeling okay?"

"Yes, I'm fine," she answered automatically.

He shot her a skeptical look before he turned to get their boarding passes. Casey covertly studied his profile. He didn't seem too well rested, either. The lines she'd noticed in his face Friday seemed to be etched even more deeply today.

As he pocketed the boarding passes, she reached down for her carry-on bag at the same time he reached for his. Their hands touched, and she drew in her breath sharply. How was she going to bear this uneasy quickening of her heartbeat at every accidental touch or casual contact?

The flight to Alaska was a long, uncomfortable one. Seated next to him, a touch away, she was more than once tempted to reach for his strong, lean hand, which rested so close to hers. Instead, she tried to move as far away as the narrow seat would allow. He had put their relationship back on a strictly professional level, and she would have to abide by his wishes.

They arrived in Anchorage in late afternoon, and the gray sky only contributed to her feelings of melancholy. A light rain was falling, and a damp chill hung in the air.

As Jeremy drove the rental car into the city, however, the photographer in Casey couldn't help but note the unique contrasts of the town, which was home to half of the state's population. The downtown area was a curious mixture of pioneer town and modern metropolis, with the half dozen or so high rises sharing space with rustic log structures.

Somehow Anchorage hadn't quite lost its frontier feel, and Casey, though fascinated by the contrasts, wasn't really surprised. The transition that Old West towns made from frontier outposts to sophisticated cities took more than a century. Anchorage, founded in 1913 as a tent city for construction workers hired to build a Federal railway, had done it in a handful of years. The result was a unique blend of yesterday, today, and tomorrow.

When they pulled up in front of the hotel, Casey began to help Jeremy unload the equipment. He stopped her with a touch on the shoulder.

"Let me. You look all in," he said gently.

"I'm fine," she insisted unsteadily, trying to still the trembling that this slight contact had set off in her limbs.

"Look, you'll only get sick if you push yourself," he said patiently. "Go ahead and check in. Maybe send for room service. But get some rest. We've got a busy week ahead of us."

She silently debated the merits of following his advice. She *was* tired. Her sleepless nights and the long flight were catching up with her. And she couldn't afford to get sick.

"Okay," she relented.

Despite the tumultuous state of her emotions, exhaustion forced her into a deep sleep. And when she awoke, refreshed after a good night's sleep, her perspective was somewhat restored. She was even able to smile when she met Jeremy for breakfast.

"You look rested," he observed. "Did you sleep well?"

"Yes, thanks." She couldn't say the same about him, though. His face looked bleak and haggard. But she made no comment.

Over breakfast they discussed their plans. Unlike Breckenridge, where they had spent most of their time apart, here they would be together, Casey concentrating on panoramic shots, Jeremy on close-up, detail shots.

Anchorage proved to be fertile ground in terms of subject matter, and they approached it from the perspective of contrasting old and new.

A day trip to Portage Glacier was fascinating. Casey gazed in awe at the huge, glacial-blue chunks of ice that floated at the base of a wall of ice. They even got to see some "calving," watching as huge chunks broke off the mass of ice with a distinctive, thunderlike rumble.

Although the day started out sunny, by early afternoon low-hanging clouds descended, casting an eerie, ominous pall over the scene. Yet the blue in the ice grew even more intense, giving the scene an ethereal beauty.

"Isn't this fabulous!" Casey exclaimed when Jeremy was within speaking distance. "I've never seen such an incredible blue! And the way the mood of this place changes! I hope we can capture it on film." Some of her old enthusiasm was back in her voice as she spoke.

"If quantity of film is any indication, then I think we're doing okay," Jeremy said with a grin.

So intent was she on her work that her relationship with Jeremy actually took second place in her mind. In fact, for a time she even forgot he was there. It wasn't until she lost her footing on some slippery rocks and felt his arm shoot out to steady her that she remembered his presence.

"Thanks!" she said shakily, realizing that she was precariously close to a sharp drop-off.

"That was close, Casey," he said with a frown. "Take it easy. Be careful."

"I will," she promised.

His arm lingered on hers longer than necessary, and she tried to read his eyes. They looked troubled. But before she could say anything else he had turned and was working his way back down the rocks. There had been a brief moment, though, when. . . . Oh, it was probably just her imagination, she told herself sharply.

They drove down to Homer, on Cook Inlet at the

tip of the Kenai Peninsula, later in the week. Casey especially enjoyed this part of the trip, for this area was less visited by tourists and, as a result, more unspoiled.

They had good weather on the way down and stopped often to take photos. The hilly, rugged terrain was covered with deep green spruce forests. Tumbling brooks were frequently seen along the roadside, and snowcapped mountains could be glimpsed in the distance. The sky was deep blue and there was a fresh scent of pine in the air. The incredible display of nature's handiwork seemed to work as a balm on her ragged nerves. She sighed deeply and leaned back in her seat.

Jeremy sent her a questioning look. "Are you all right?"

"Yes. Just enjoying this gorgeous scenery."

"It's pretty spectacular," he agreed.

"Homer is where we should charter a floatplane," she said, consulting her notes. "Dan said the view of the glaciers near the town at sunset is spectacular."

"That sounds good."

He made no further comment, and Casey glanced over at him. He'd been reticent and preoccupied much of the time since they'd arrived in Alaska. A surge of despair washed over her, and she spoke before she could stop the words:

"Jeremy, what's the matter? Ever since you saw me with Dan you've withdrawn into yourself. You're just the way you were when we first met—polite and businesslike, but distant. Did I do something wrong? Were you upset because I was with Dan? Can't you be honest with me?'' The desperation and confusion in her voice were obvious.

Jeremy seemed momentarily taken aback by her outburst, and there was a long pause before he replied. When he did, he seemed to be weighing his response, choosing each word carefully.

''No. You didn't do anything wrong,'' he said so softly that she had to lean close to hear him. In his voice, unguarded for a moment, she heard a regret and hopelessness that pulled at her heart. But when he continued, his tone was more controlled. ''Seeing you with Dan just made me take another look at our relationship. It's just not right, Casey. I don't know what else to say.''

The finality in his voice told her not to harbor any hope of recapturing their closeness, and she was filled with a deep ache of sadness.

''Then I guess there's nothing else *to* say,'' she said quietly, with a dignity and composure that surprised her. She wouldn't force her attentions on someone who didn't want her. Turning away, she stared out the window for the rest of the trip, her eyes now blind to the spectacular scenery.

They went up in the floatplane that evening in Homer, as Casey had suggested, but the beauty of the scene barely penetrated her consciousness. She was hardly aware of the volcano in the harbor, silhouetted against a multicolored sunset, or the ice on the glacier-encrusted mountains, ice that sparkled like diamonds as the last rays of the setting sun fleetingly touched it. She automatically took photos, but the magnificent scene captured in her viewfinder didn't even register in her mind.

The ride ended shortly thereafter with a gentle touch of the plane's pontoons on the water. She and Jeremy ate a quiet dinner, which she had difficulty swallowing, and then they parted for the night.

A ringing phone awakened Casey at five in the morning, and she groggily reached for it, muttering a sleepy "hello" into the mouthpiece.

"Casey, it's Jeremy. I think we'd better head back to Anchorage. They're predicting snow, and we could get stuck. If we leave within the next hour, we might miss it."

In her half-awake condition, Casey didn't fully comprehend his statement. But the word *snow* penetrated her consciousness.

"Snow?" she repeated. "In May?"

"This is Alaska," he reminded her. "And it's still early spring. But this is a bit unusual. It came up very suddenly. Can you be ready to leave in half an hour?"

"Yes." She was already sitting up. "I'll meet you in the lobby."

Thirty minutes later, her small overnight bag in

hand, Casey stepped into the lobby. It was still dark, but there was an oppressiveness in the air that almost tangibly spoke of a storm. The temperature had dropped, too, and she shivered.

"I've already paid the bill," Jeremy said as he walked toward her and took her small case. He led her out the door and stowed her bag quickly in the backseat. "Are you going to be warm enough?" he asked with a frown, eyeing her thin nylon windbreaker.

"This is all I brought. It was nice when we left yesterday."

"Well, the car will be warm. I'm glad we have front-wheel drive."

It grew light shortly after they left—or as light as it was going to get. Heavy, gray, snow-laden clouds hung low, obscuring the mountain peaks that yesterday had been etched so brilliantly against the sky. Soon large, feathery flakes began to waft to the ground.

Casey cast a worried look at the sky. This reminded her of the drive to Breckenridge—except this time they were in a much more remote area.

The snow quickly increased in intensity, and soon the road and the surrounding countryside were blanketed in white. Only one car passed them in two hours. The wind had picked up as well, and Casey knew that Jeremy was struggling to keep the car on the road. A frown furrowed his brow, and this added to her unease, for Jeremy was usually calm in situations like this. If he was worried, there was just cause.

Suddenly the car swerved, and Casey caught a quick glimpse of a large animal as it darted in front of the vehicle. She stifled a scream as the car careened across the road, and then she felt it slipping on the pavement. She closed her eyes and gripped the edge of the dashboard, her body rigid with fear.

For an eternity the car seemed to fishtail across the icy surface. But at last, with a sickening thud, it came to rest in the ditch at the edge of the road. The car was tilted up in the front, and only Casey's grip on the dashboard kept her from falling back against the seat.

"Casey! Casey, are you all right?"

Slowly she opened her eyes. Jeremy was looking at her intently, as if trying to assess her condition, and his face was as strained and white as her own. She forced herself to nod.

"Let go of the dashboard, Casey," he cajoled gently, prying her fingers free. Carefully she released them.

Jeremy pulled her trembling body into his arms and held her, murmuring soothing words, and she clung to him. The sinewy strength of his hands and the firm leanness of him were the most convincing reassurances that the nightmare was over.

At last her trembling subsided and he pulled away, searching her face with concern. "Okay now?"

She nodded and smiled shakily. "What happened? I thought I saw a deer dart in front of the car."

"I think it was a moose. Not that it matters. The result is the same." With a sudden violence that startled her he hit the dashboard with his fist. "I shouldn't even have attempted this drive. We might have been killed."

"We weren't. Besides, you didn't know the storm was going to be this bad."

"I'll take a look at the damage," he said, self-reproach still evident in his voice.

He opened the door and an icy blast of air entered, immediately chilling the warm car. Casey shivered and wrapped her arms around her body. Jeremy frowned.

"If you've got any extra clothes, put them on," he instructed. "We might be here for a while."

As soon as he closed the door, Casey reached behind the seat and rummaged through her small overnight case. The only useful article of clothing was a flannel shirt, and she put this on over her cotton blouse. Then she zipped up her windbreaker. It wasn't much of an improvement.

She peered out the window but couldn't see more than a foot through the white curtain of snow. She heard Jeremy open the trunk, though, and a few minutes later he got back in the car. He was covered with snow, and she helped him brush it off.

"We're definitely stuck," he said in disgust. "There's no way we're going to get out of here on our own. I set a flare on the road, but I doubt if anyone will be out on a day like this. We may have a long wait."

Casey jammed her hands in the pockets of her windbreaker as she faced this bleak prospect. She knew without being told that their greatest problem was the cold. The gas in the car would last only so long, and when it was gone, so was their heater.

Jeremy had been watching her face, and when he spoke it was in a carefully controlled matter-of-fact tone.

"I can see you've already realized that the cold is our worst enemy. I'll turn the engine on every fifteen minutes to warm up the car, but we may be here a long time. I don't want to use up the gas any faster than necessary. So we're going to have to rely on body heat to provide the extra warmth."

She gave him a suspicious look. "What do you mean?"

"You've heard the term 'snuggle'? It's not very scientific, but it works."

Casey moved even farther away into her corner of the seat. She couldn't bear to be that close to him, knowing how he felt about her. "I don't think that's such a good idea."

"Do you have a better one?"

She didn't answer.

"Look, Casey, it's the only practical solution."

She couldn't argue with his logic, so she remained silent.

"I don't like this any better than you do," he continued, as if he thought that remark would make her feel better. "This is just as hard for me as it is for you. Come on over."

She knew he had won. It would be foolish and childish to argue with him. Slowly she edged across the seat toward him, her eyes on his fingers as he unbuttoned his jacket. He slipped his right arm out of the sleeve and motioned for her to move closer. She did so with trepidation, making sure that she wasn't in body contact with him.

"Casey, if this is going to work, we've got to be a lot closer." Without waiting for her to respond, he put his arm around her and pulled her toward him until the sides of their bodies met from shoulder to ankle. Then he pulled his coat around her shoulder.

She stiffened. If only he knew how difficult it was for her to be this close to him! She could hear the steady beat of his heart beneath his muscular chest as she leaned against him, and her breathing became erratic. She sat rigidly in his arms until at last she heard him exclaim something under his breath.

"For heaven's sake, relax, Casey! If you sit there stiff as a board, we're both going to be uncomfortable.

You may find being close to me disagreeable, but it's better than the alternative.''

As he spoke, the warmth of his body was seeping into her, and she found her muscles relaxing of their own accord. In fact, as the minutes ticked by, she grew so relaxed that she found her eyelids growing heavy. Sleepily, hardly aware of what she was doing, she snuggled even closer to Jeremy in the warm cocoon they'd created.

Within a few minutes she was asleep, and her head dropped to his shoulder, her hair cascading down his shirt. She didn't see him reach over and gently lift a few of the silky strands, fingering them tenderly as she slept. And she didn't see the regret in his eyes.

A long time later, a shout awakened Casey, and she opened her eyes to find that the snow had stopped. Sleepily, she stretched.

"I think help has arrived," Jeremy said, nodding toward the road. Carefully he extricated himself and opened the car door, and Casey immediately missed the warmth of his body next to hers. She peered outside and saw him confering with a young man in a truck, and a few moments later he came back to the car.

"He can't pull the car out, but he's on his way to Anchorage and will give us a lift," he said.

"Okay." She gathered up her belongings, and with Jeremy's arm protectively under her elbow, made her way to the truck.

"Hi. I'm Joe," the young man greeted her with a grin. He was dressed in a wool cap, boots, and a heavy jacket—obviously a native, she thought wryly. "I was just telling your husband, you folks were sure lucky. That was some storm!"

Casey didn't bother to correct him about their marital status, and neither did Jeremy.

Joe chatted amiably on the way back to Anchorage, and Casey let Jeremy carry the bulk of the conversation. She was emotionally exhausted from their close call.

Joe dropped them off at their hotel, but refused to let them compensate him for his trouble.

"Heck, Alaskans are always glad to help their neighbors," he said with a grin.

They watched him drive away, and then Jeremy turned to Casey.

"You look worn out. Why don't you make it an early night? We've got a long flight home tomorrow."

"I think that's a good idea," she agreed readily.

As she turned away, his arm restrained her. "Are you sure you're all right, Casey?" Concern colored his voice.

"Yes. Just a bit shaky. I'll be okay after a good night's sleep."

"You know, you told me when I hired you that you were sturdier than you looked," he said quietly. "I didn't really believe it then. I do now."

She looked at him, surprised at that unexpected remark. She didn't know how to respond.

Apparently he didn't expect an answer, for he simply took her arm and led her to her room, where he left her at the door. Normally she would have mulled over a comment like that, but not tonight. She was tired, and all she wanted to do was sleep.

Once under the warm covers, though, she found sleep elusive. Her thoughts kept turning to Jeremy. She recalled their day at the farm, when she'd thought her heart would burst with happiness. That scene seemed destined never to be repeated.

As sleep finally came, her last conscious thought was a plea. *Please make Jeremy realize how much I care for him. Make him love me as I love him.*

Chapter Eleven

 B ut her plea went unanswered, and with each day that passed Casey's spirits sank lower. Her hopes for a romantic relationship with Jeremy withered and died. Even her pleasure in her job began to diminish. The travel lost its glamour as one lonely hotel room began to blur into another. She started to think seriously about looking for another position.

One day she returned early from lunch, hoping to respond to some urgent correspondence without many interruptions. The connecting door between her office and Jeremy's was partially open, and a short time after she returned she heard him enter. She needed to talk with him about one letter, but she hated to intrude on his lunch hour, though he rarely took an ''official'' lunch break. As she debated, she heard a soft knock on his door.

''Come in,'' he called.

The door opened, and Casey heard a woman's hesitant voice.

"Hello, Jeremy." The voice faltered, as if the speaker was uncertain of her welcome.

Silence greeted the woman's words, and Casey frowned. Why didn't Jeremy return the greeting? His manners were usually impeccable.

At last she heard him rise, and when he spoke she was shocked by the tense, strained timbre of his voice.

"Hello, Connie. This is a surprise."

"I'm sure it is. The receptionist must be at lunch, or I would have asked her to call and let you know I was here. May I come in?"

"Of course."

Connie? Why did that name ring a bell? And then it dawned on her. Connie was the name of Jeremy's ex-fiancée. But what could she want?

From where she sat, Casey could glimpse the chair across from Jeremy's desk, and a moment later a slim blond woman seated herself there and elegantly crossed her legs. She was dressed in a beautifully cut suit of deep lavender and a white blouse with frilly cuffs and lace at the throat. She had a fair complexion, and her hair, chin-length and stylishly turned under, was smooth and shiny.

The woman was definitely attractive, and Casey felt a twinge of . . . jealousy? It was an unfamiliar emotion, and she had a hard time putting a name to the mixture of anger, fear, and pain that unexpectedly rushed over her.

As the visitor nervously twisted her hands in her lap, Casey quickly moved back out of sight. She didn't want to be caught staring or eavesdropping. But how could she make a graceful exit?

Jeremy hadn't spoken since the woman entered, but now he cleared his throat.

"What can I do for you, Connie?" He was now back in control, and his tone was friendly but cool.

"I'm sorry to bother you, Jeremy. I know I'm probably the last person you want to see. But I thought it was only right to tell you in person rather than let you read it in the paper. After all, we were . . . very close, once."

"Tell me what?"

"That I'm getting married."

Casey heard a sharp snap, as if a pencil had been broken in two. But when Jeremy spoke, his voice was matter-of-fact. "I see."

"I'm truly sorry about everything, Jeremy," Connie continued. "I loved you once, you know." She sniffed, and Casey could imagine her dabbing at her eyes with a lace-edged handkerchief. "It was just, well . . . you know."

"I know." Casey heard the resignation in his voice. Then he sighed. "It's okay, Connie. It's over. Life has gone on."

Casey squirmed uncomfortably. This was definitely

a private conversation. But she'd waited so long now that she couldn't very well get up and leave. The only way out was past the adjoining door to Jeremy's office, and he was sure to see her. She should have left as soon as Connie entered.

"I wish you every happiness, Connie."

"Thank you. You always were gallant. If only. . . ." Connie left the sentence unfinished, her voice tinged with regret.

"We can't live our lives with 'ifs,' " Jeremy told her, as Casey fumed inwardly at the woman's insensitivity. "But I appreciate your coming by. I know it was hard for you."

"It was the least I could do. I always felt bad about the way it ended. Well, then . . . ." Casey heard her rise, the relief in her voice evident. It was obvious that she had considered this visit a duty, and she was glad it was over. "Oh, no, Jeremy, stay there. No need for you to get up," she said, her voice edged with panic.

So she couldn't bear to be reminded of his limp even now, Casey thought. How could she be so shallow, letting something so inconsequential affect her feelings for Jeremy?

Suddenly the woman was in Casey's line of vision again, moving toward the door.

"Good-bye, Jeremy."

"Good-bye, Connie. And good luck."

Casey heard the outer door close and she held her

breath, waiting. Then she heard Jeremy flip the switch on the light table, and she groaned inwardly. Sometimes he spent hours there!

Could she edge past the door without being seen? It was doubtful. The light table was placed in such a way that he had a clear view of her door. Well, she'd just have to sit it out and hope he would leave the office before too long.

She turned carefully to reach for a book behind her, but despite her caution, her elbow knocked off the jar of peppermints she always kept on the corner of her desk. She watched helplessly, in horror, as it fell. It almost seemed to be happening in slow motion.

As the jar smashed to the floor, Casey's heart flew to her throat. What would Jeremy think?

She didn't have to wait long for the answer to her question. Within moments he appeared on the threshold, a frown on his face.

Casey stared at him, flinching under his cold gaze. She couldn't blame him for his anger and embarrassment. In his place, she would feel the same way.

"I'm sorry, Jeremy," she said contritely, the color rising in her cheeks. "I didn't mean to eavesdrop. By the time I realized it was a personal conversation, it was too late to get out gracefully."

Suddenly, unexpectedly, his shoulders sagged, and he ran a hand through his hair.

"It's okay. I know you well enough to know you'd never purposely listen to a private conversation."

Casey was relieved that his anger had dissipated so rapidly. In fact, as he stood at the door, his hands shoved into his pockets, he seemed to want to say more, but she sensed that he didn't know how to begin.

"I take it that was your ex-fiancée?" she ventured uncertainly.

"Yes. As I'm sure you heard, she's getting married."

"I'm sorry, Jeremy."

"Don't be. Any feelings I had for her are long gone."

"Are you sure?" Casey asked quietly.

He frowned. "What do you mean?"

"Well, something is holding you back from getting involved with anyone else. I thought maybe you still cared for her, even after what she did to you."

"No. It was just a shock, seeing her after all this time," he said, ignoring her comment about starting a new relationship. "I take it you've heard the story of my accident and broken engagement."

"Mike told me when I first started." Casey paused, and then impulsively continued. "Connie made a terrible mistake when she walked out on you. I don't know how you can forgive her."

"She didn't mean to hurt me. Most people just aren't comfortable around those with physical disabilities. Connie can't help how she feels."

"Oh, for heaven's sake, Jeremy! How can you

defend her?'' Casey asked in exasperation. ''What she did was immature and selfish. Why should a minor physical defect make any difference at all in the way a person feels? Trite as it may sound, it's what's inside that matters.''

''Do you really believe that?'' he asked quietly.

''Of course I do.''

''Let's just suppose, then, that I was in love with you,'' he said carefully, and Casey's breath caught in her throat. ''What right would I have to ask you to marry me, knowing I could never share so much of your life? I can't play tennis. I can't ski. I can't dance. I can't even jog,'' he said in disgust.

''Do you really think those things are that important?'' she asked, choosing her words carefully. ''Just look at all the things you can do.''

''It's not that simple,'' he said with a sigh, apparently hearing the words, but not the message. When he spoke again, his voice was thoughtful. ''Actually, I should probably be grateful to Connie. She made me realize that anyone who shared my life would be deprived of so many experiences. For me to expect someone to make that sacrifice would be selfish. Your words sound good, Casey. And I know you believe them. But *saying* that a disability doesn't make any difference is one thing. *Living* with it is another.''

She looked at him in silence for a moment before she spoke, her eyes bright with tears.

''You say you've come to terms with your disability, but you haven't. Maybe you've accepted the physical reality of it, but you haven't accepted it emotionally. If you had, you'd realize how irrelevant it is. I know you had a bad experience with Connie. But her response to what happened to you wasn't the response of a mature, reasonable person. And yet that's how you're treating it. There will always be people in this world who can't look beyond the physical reality of your limp, who can't deal with it. But that's their problem, Jeremy, not yours. And until you learn that, and accept it, you're not really living. You're blocking people out, and you're throwing away love.''

Casey knew she was fighting a losing battle. She could see it in his eyes.

''I'm sorry, Casey,'' was all he said.

''I know,'' she snapped, throwing away caution. She had nothing to lose now by being honest. Their relationship was dead, anyway. ''For yourself. Well, wake up, Mr. Morgan. You're a gifted photographer with a fine mind and—buried somewhere, I think— a loving and compassionate heart. Your life should be full of hope, not despair. You think you're being so noble by not getting involved in a relationship. Well, deep down I think that nobility is just another way of feeling sorry for yourself.''

His face had taken on a ruddy color, and she knew he was angry. But she didn't care. Someone needed to shake him up.

"Those are pretty hard words," he said, his voice strained. "It's easy to talk. But do you have any idea what it's like to have your life radically changed in the blink of an eye? To suddenly find that you can't do things you've taken for granted all your life? That's bad enough. But how would you like to have someone you love walk out on you? That's not so easy to cope with. And how would you like to wonder, every time someone is nice to you, whether it's because they genuinely like you or because they pity you?"

"Jeremy Morgan, the only pity in this room is the pity you feel for yourself!" she said furiously. She paused and took a deep breath, and when she spoke again the anger in her voice had been replaced with sadness. "No, I take that back. I do feel sorry for you. Not because of your leg, but because of what you've let that do to your life. You are a cripple, Jeremy—an emotional cripple."

Her words were brutally honest, and she saw a spasm of pain pass over his face, almost as if he'd been physically struck. Her heart went out to him, and she wanted to take him in her arms and tell him she loved him as she had never loved anyone before. But he had already made it clear that her love was not wanted.

She rose and brushed past him, stumbling as she did so. His arm instinctively shot out to steady her, but she shrugged him off violently and continued into the hall. She had to get out of here! She couldn't face

Jeremy again today. In fact, she wasn't sure if she could face him ever again. She'd said some terrible things to him. But something inside her had snapped, and there was no going back.

When Casey arrived home she mechanically fixed herself a cup of tea and then sat down, forcing herself to think about the situation logically. After her outburst, Jeremy might very well fire her. And he would certainly be within his rights. She had said things that would make a working relationship impossible.

The more she thought about it, the more certain she became that Jeremy would let her go. She had seen his white, shocked face as she left the room. Perhaps she should make it easier on everyone and simply quit. Now that there was no hope of salvaging their relationship, it seemed pointlessly painful to prolong their contact.

She decided to sleep on the decision, for she wanted to be sure that she was doing the right thing and not simply overreacting because of the emotionalism of the situation. But when she awoke the next morning after a restless night, she felt more convinced than ever that the only course of action open to her was to resign.

Casey didn't have to worry about facing Jeremy, because she knew he was leaving on an assignment that morning. So as soon as she cleared up the business that had accumulated during her absence the day before, she rang Mike and asked to see him.

"Sure, come on down," he invited.

Casey took a deep breath to steady her pounding heart before she entered Mike's office. She fully realized what a wonderful opportunity she was giving up. Working on *Journeys* had been a dream job, and she knew it. But that dream had turned into a nightmare. There was no choice now but to move on, and her experience here would be a great asset in the job search ahead of her.

"It's good to see you," Mike said. "You're on the go so much our paths rarely cross. Jeremy's just as bad. I haven't really talked to him in weeks. Is something wrong, Casey?" he asked, noting the shadow that crossed her face at the mention of Jeremy's name.

"I'm not sure exactly how to tell you this, Mike, without seeming ungrateful for the wonderful opportunity you've given me here. It's been a tremendous experience. But I . . . I'm going to have to resign."

Mike's usually placid face registered surprise and disbelief.

"Resign?" he echoed. "Are you serious? I thought you enjoyed your job here."

"I do. Or I did," she amended. "This doesn't have anything to do with the job itself. It's a . . . personal matter."

"Personal matter?" Mike said with a frown.

Casey shifted uncomfortably. "It's just that, well, Jeremy and I have had a serious . . . misunderstanding . . . and it's strained our relationship. I just don't feel comfortable working with him anymore, and I'm sure he feels the same way."

Casey hoped Mike wouldn't press for details. It was painful enough to have to admit this much. Fortunately, he seemed to recognize her feelings, for his next question was put very gently. "I take it this isn't something you want to discuss?"

"No. I'm sorry, Mike. It would serve no purpose."

"And you're sure you can't stay with us? *Journeys* will feel your loss."

"Thank you. But no. It would be impossible."

Mike sighed. "Okay. You certainly are in a better position than I to make that judgment."

"I'd like to leave as soon as possible," she said. "But of course I'll stay until you find a replacement, if you think that's necessary."

Mike shook his head. "I don't want to make it hard on you. "How long would it take you to wrap up the projects you're involved in now?"

She did some quick mental calculations. "About a week."

"Then I won't force you to stay any longer than that."

"Thank you, Mike," she said gratefully.

"That's all right. Would you like me to tell Jeremy?"

"Would you? I suppose I'm being a coward, but it really would be easier on me."

"Of course. He'll be back on Monday, won't he?"

"Yes."

"Why not make that your last day?" he said, consulting his calendar. Then he turned to her with a smile, his voice tinged with regret. "We're going to miss you, Casey."

"The feeling is mutual," she admitted, close to tears. "I can't thank you enough for this opportunity. I'm sorry things didn't work out differently."

"So am I. But we're glad we had you this long. You know, of course, that I wish you only the best. And I'll be glad to give you a recommendation."

"Thanks, Mike. I'll probably take you up on that."

Casey moved in a daze through the remainder of the week. It was almost as if this part of her life was already over. The only thing that remained was a final confrontation with Jeremy, and she dreaded that.

Seated at her desk Monday morning, filled with nervous apprehension, she didn't even try to work. She just mechanically cleaned out her files, sorting through the amazing amount of material that she had accumulated over the last few months.

She knew that Mike would speak to Jeremy immediately, and that he would probably then confront her. What would his reaction be to her departure? she wondered. Anger? Relief? Surprise? Probably good riddance, after their last encounter, she thought bitterly.

She heard his door open, and she stiffened. A quick glance at her watch told her that he'd been with Mike for only about fifteen minutes. She tried to force her heart to slow its rapid pounding. A few deep breaths helped a little, but she sat rigidly in her chair, her eyes locked on the closed connecting door between their offices.

She waited expectantly for it to open, but as the minutes slipped by it remained closed. She frowned. Was her departure so inconsequential to Jeremy that he wasn't even going to speak to her about it?

At last, puzzled and disheartened, she went back to cleaning out her desk.

Some time later, her thoughts in the past as she fingered the Breckenridge itinerary she'd kept in her files, she heard the knob of the adjoining door turn. Her eyes flew up, and she gripped the arm of her chair with her free hand as Jeremy stepped through the opening.

Her first thought was that he looked old. Not just in body, but in spirit. She looked into his eyes, expecting to see reproach, anger, or cool indifference. Instead she saw only an infinite sadness, so empty and hopeless that it made her heart weep. He ran a hand through his hair, an endearingly familiar gesture, and she realized before he jammed it into his pocket that he was trembling, just as she was.

She looked at him, a wistful sadness in her eyes as she mourned for something that could never be. They could have been happy together, she knew. If only Jeremy had realized that too.

He stayed in the doorway for a long moment, his eyes fixed on her, as if he were memorizing her every feature. Her own eyes dropped under his scrutiny. Why didn't he say something?

When he did attempt to speak, his voice seemed to fail, for he had to clear his throat and start again. "Mike told me that you're leaving."

She nodded without looking up. "Yes. It seemed the best thing."

"You're probably right." But he didn't sound convinced. Then he sighed. "We have made a mess of things, haven't we, Casey?" he said gently.

"I guess so," she whispered. She didn't know how else to respond. She had been prepared to face his anger, but not this disheartened sadness.

"We did have some good times, though."

"Yes." She thought about Breckenridge and about their day on the farm, when life had seemed to hold the promise of love. Her eyes began to fill with tears, and she struggled to keep them from spilling out.

"What will you do now?" he asked.

"I—I'm not sure. I haven't really thought about it. Mom and Dad asked me to come home for a vacation, and I agreed."

He nodded. "That's a good idea." He straightened

up with an effort, as if he wasn't sure whether he could stay on his feet without the support of the door-frame.

Casey's eyes, wide and imploring, looked at him hungrily, trying to impress on her mind every contour of his face. But it wasn't really necessary. She knew that she would carry his image with her for the rest of her life.

"Can I buy you lunch on your last day?" he offered.

"Thanks. But Molly and I already have plans." She wanted desperately to say yes, but why prolong the strain on her emotions? It would serve no purpose.

"I see. Well, don't feel you have to stay all day. I have an appointment this afternoon, so I'll say good-bye now."

He walked over to her and reached for her hand. She stretched it out to him, but instead of shaking it he cupped it between his hands. His long, lean fingers gently squeezed hers.

"I'm not sorry we met, Casey," he said softly. "I hope you're not, either. And in case I haven't told you, you're a wonderful photographer. If there's ever anything I can do to help you, please call me."

"Thank you, Jeremy." Her voice was shaking and her eyes were suspiciously moist.

He held her hand for a long moment before letting it go with apparent reluctance. Then he turned suddenly and strode away, shutting the door between their offices without a backward glance.

So that was it, she thought bleakly. The end of a ... what? A job? In reality, except for a few brief encounters, that was all there was between them. But the ache in her heart told her that there could have been so much more.

After a subdued lunch with Molly, Casey returned to her office. It was bare, just as it had been the day she entered it for the first time. It was almost as if she'd never been here, she thought, and a wave of depression swept over her.

Then, impatient with herself for her melancholy, she resolutely gathered up her few remaining belongings. Without looking back, she moved quickly through the door and walked away.

Chapter Twelve

Casey's parents welcomed her home with understanding and love, and in that atmosphere of concern and care she slowly began to regain her equilibrium.

It wasn't until a few days after her arrival, though, that she felt able to talk about all that had happened. Her parents hadn't pushed her to discuss her reasons for quitting her job, although she knew they were very curious. But finally, as she and her mother sat in the garden one evening, she told her the story.

"I'm so sorry," Amanda said when Casey finished, her voice distressed. "I know how much you hoped that something would come of that relationship. I wish it had turned out differently."

"So do I. But love can't be forced. Jeremy just isn't ready for another relationship, I guess. And besides," Casey added with a sigh, "I'm not really sure how he felt about me. I thought he cared, but after all that's happened, I don't know anymore.''

As the days passed, Casey kept waiting for the ache in her heart to ease. But it didn't. She tried to put thoughts of Jeremy out of her mind, but her efforts were unsuccessful. Frequently, in the middle of a conversation, a word would trigger some memory of him and her mind would travel back in time. Then, when a question was asked of her, she'd have to admit that she hadn't been listening.

What she needed was something to occupy her thoughts, to keep her so busy that she didn't have time to think of Jeremy. It would probably be a good idea to start looking for another job, to think about the future.

Unfortunately, a future without Jeremy didn't seem to hold much promise. But she'd have to get over that attitude. She had been hard on him for letting a bad experience ruin his life. Maybe she should take her own advice.

These were her thoughts late one Saturday afternoon during the second week of her visit. She was lying in a chaise longue in the yard, an unopened book in her lap, her eyes closed. The warm breeze was soothing, and birds were chirping in the tree above her. It was so restful here, so comfortable and familiar. . . . She was just beginning to drift to sleep when her mother's voice brought her back to reality.

''Casey, are you out here?''

Her eyes flew open. "Yes. I'm over here."

"Oh. Sorry, dear. I didn't mean to disturb you, but I wanted to tell you that your father and I are leaving now for the Gottliebs' dinner party, and Rob will be at Cindy's all evening. Will you be okay?"

Ever since she'd returned, Amanda had hovered over her like a mother hen, reminding Casey of the days when she'd been a little girl and misplaced some special toy or had the sniffles. A tender smile curved her lips.

"Of course, Mom," she assured her. "Don't worry."

"Well, I hate to leave you alone," Amanda said worriedly.

"I have a good book to read. I'll enjoy the evening. You just have a good time."

"Well . . . I left some cookies on the counter if you get hungry later. And there's lemonade in the refrigerator."

"Thanks, Mom."

Casey watched her parents leave, arm in arm, laughing and chatting like teenagers. What a special relationship they had. Would she ever find love like that? With Jeremy out of her life, the prospects seemed bleak.

To lift her drooping spirits, she decided to take her book out to the summerhouse. It had been one of her favorite places as a child, and she'd spent hours there, imagining one time that it was a castle, another time, a ship. It was at the very back of the yard, surrounded by shrubs and trees, and it had always seemed to be a special place, apart from the world.

Casey poured a glass of lemonade and then headed for the screened-in, gazebolike structure. Seating herself in the swing that hung on one side, she tucked her legs under her and opened the book. Within minutes she was absorbed in a suspense tale by one of her favorite authors.

Eventually it grew dark, and automatically she switched on the light. She continued to read as the crickets chirped and the fireflies buzzed around her little oasis of light.

Casey wasn't sure how long she had been sitting there when she suddenly sensed another presence. She looked up, but there didn't appear to be anyone there. She was just about to resume reading when her eye was caught by what seemed to be a shadowy figure lurking just beyond the light that spilled from the summerhouse.

"Is anyone there?" she asked, frowning, a tingle of fear running along her spine. She had never worried about the seclusion of the summerhouse before, but suddenly she was apprehensive about being there alone.

The figure disengaged itself from the bushes and moved slightly forward, but the shadows were still too strong for her to identify the person.

"It's me, Casey."

Casey's heart seemed to stop beating for an instant, and then it rushed on. She knew that voice. Oh, how well she knew that voice! It had haunted her dreams for months.

''Jeremy?'' she asked incredulously.

''Yes.'' He moved into the light, and her eyes drank in the sight of him. ''I'm sorry if I frightened you. I've been standing here for a long time, trying to get up the courage to talk to you.''

''How did you find me, way back here?''

''You told me once that this was one of your favorite spots. When no one answered the bell, I thought maybe you'd be here.''

Casey just stared at him in confusion. What was he doing here? And why did he seem so ill at ease?

''May I come in?'' he asked finally. His voice was uncertain, nervous. She had never before seen this side of the confident, self-assured Jeremy Morgan.

''Yes, of course.''

He came forward, and she suddenly realized that he was holding the biggest bouquet she'd ever seen.

''These are for you,'' he said, holding them out to her when he was inside. ''I tried to find lilacs, but they said it was the wrong season. So I had to settle for that.'' He pointed to a silk spray of lilacs in the center of the bouquet.

''Thank you,'' she said, cradling the flowers in her arms. ''They're lovely.''

There was an awkward pause, and then Jeremy cleared his throat and spoke again.

"I guess you're wondering why I'm here."

"Well, that thought *had* crossed my mind," she admitted, her eyes cautious. Maybe Mike had sent him to try to lure her back to the magazine. Or maybe he wanted their parting to be on friendlier terms, and this was his way of making peace. She stared at him, waiting for him to continue.

"Do you mind if I sit down?" he asked.

"No, of course not."

He chose a wicker chair across from her, but he didn't relax against its plump cushions. Instead, he sat on the edge of the chair, hunched over, his elbows resting on his knees, rubbing his hands together.

For Casey, the scene had a strange unreality about it. The sweet-smelling flowers were real enough—she had them in her arms—but it was hard to believe that Jeremy was actually sitting across from her. She looked at his face, which was haggard and tired, and watched as he ran his hand through his hair in an all-too-familiar gesture.

"I really don't know where to begin, Casey," he said at last. "I thought I knew exactly what I wanted to say, and now it all sounds wrong."

She waited, giving him time to collect his thoughts. She was still puzzled about this visit, and taken aback by Jeremy's unfamiliar manner. He seemed a little awkward and tongue-tied—like a teenager on his first date. He closed his eyes for a minute, the frown lines between them deepening perceptibly. Then he looked at her, and she saw . . . fear? . . . pain? . . . uncertainty? . . . in their depths. She couldn't identify the emotion. All she knew for sure was that he was troubled.

"Is something wrong at the magazine?" she asked finally.

"No. This has nothing to do with *Journeys*," he said. "It has to do with us."

"Us?" she repeated in surprise.

"Yes, us."

"There is no 'us,' Jeremy," she said quietly.

He stood suddenly, jammed his hands in his pockets, and began to pace in the confined space.

"I know. But I think there could have been. I think I threw something very precious away, and I'm terrified that it's too late to recapture it."

Casey forced down the hope that rose within her. She'd been misled once before, when she had thought he cared. She looked at him silently, her skepticism clearly reflected in her eyes.

"Oh, Casey! I'm so sorry," he blurted out suddenly, his voice so filled with pain and remorse that it tore at her heart. "I don't blame you for being cautious. I gave you one set of signals, and then all of a sudden, in midstream, I changed course without even having the consideration to tell you why. And all the time I thought I was doing it for you, that I was saving you from a fate you'd live to regret,'' he said in disgust.

She leaned over and carefully set the flowers on the glass-topped table next to her.

''You can sit next to me, if you like,'' she said quietly.

He was beside her in an instant, and the gratitude in his eyes was touching. She looked up at him, longing to ask so many questions. But she held them in check for the moment. Jeremy clearly had more to say, and she wanted to hear every word.

''After you left,'' he continued, ''I had a lot of time to think about our last conversation. I guess sometimes people are too close to their own situation to see it clearly. But you opened my eyes. Everything you said that day was true. I hadn't come to grips with my limp on an emotional level. I don't know— maybe I didn't want to. Maybe it was a convenient excuse not to risk commitment. I guess I was afraid to let myself love you, Casey. I didn't want to be hurt again. Even though I now realize that you would never have hurt me. If anyone has done the hurting in this relationship, it's been me.''

For the first time, he had mentioned the word *love*, and Casey's heart leaped.

''Are you saying that you . . . that you care for me, Jeremy?'' she asked cautiously. She wanted to believe what she was hearing, but she, too, was afraid.

"I'm saying more than that. I'm saying that I love you."

She stared at him mutely, unable to respond. The words she'd longed to hear had been spoken, but so many questions remained.

"Why didn't you ever tell me?" she asked at last.

"I didn't think it was fair to ask you to tie yourself to a man who wasn't physically sound," he said. "I'll admit that my resolve wavered for a time. I simply couldn't resist you. But when I saw you dancing with Dan Green that night, I decided I was being selfish. I thought you deserved a man who had no physical defects."

"But I told you how I felt about that."

"I know. I guess I wasn't really listening, not with my heart. I couldn't believe that you could look beyond my limp and love me for who I am, when even I couldn't do that for myself."

"And now?" she asked.

"For the first time, I truly feel that I've accepted the limp on all levels," he said with conviction. "I feel at peace with it."

"I'm glad, Jeremy," she said sincerely. "Maybe now you can move forward with your life."

"That's really why I'm here." He reached over and plucked the spray of silk lilacs out of the center of the bouquet, fingering them as he spoke. "You told me once that you love lilacs because their fragrance always makes you think of spring and of new beginnings. I was hoping that we could make a new start tonight.'' He paused and took a deep breath. ''I want to marry you, Casey, if you'll have me. Not right away,'' he hastened to add after noting the quick flash of emotions that played across her face. ''You need time to think, and we need time to get to know each other better. But I just want you to know that marriage with the most wonderful woman I've ever met is my ultimate goal. No more pretending. I've decided that honesty is the best policy.''

Casey's reserve and caution had been melting away during Jeremy's speech, and now tears glistened in her eyes.

''I never meant to hurt you, Casey,'' he said fervently. ''I wouldn't blame you if you didn't forgive me. But when you left, I suddenly realized that I didn't want to live without you. That I *couldn't* live without you. You bring such warmth and happiness to my life. When you left, I felt as if the sunshine had gone out of my life.'' He paused and took a deep breath. ''I know I'm asking a lot, but do you think . . . do you think we could give it another try?''

''Oh, Jeremy! I've waited so long to hear you say all this,'' she said, a sob catching in her throat. ''I can't believe it's really happening now.''

She saw the look of relief wash across his face, and the tense lines around his eyes and mouth eased.

''Does that mean you'll forgive me? That you're willing to give it another try?''

"Yes. I love you, Jeremy. I've loved you for so long it seems like forever."

He reached for her trembling hands and smiled at her with such infinite tenderness that her throat constricted and she found it difficult to breathe. He stroked her hair and pulled her close, and she realized that he was trembling too.

"Oh, my darling, do you have any idea how much I love you?" he asked, his voice hoarse with emotion.

"It can't be more than I love you," she whispered.

He pulled away from her enough to capture her lips in a sweet, tender kiss. Then his lips moved downward, gently brushing against the curve of her neck. She melted against him with a sigh, and his lips moved back to hers. As his kiss deepened, a long, sweet shiver of delight ran through her.

Casey felt a sense of joy and wholeness that she had never envisioned, and she responded with an ardor that she hadn't known she possessed.

The kiss went on for a long time, and it was Jeremy who finally pulled away.

"I think we'd better call a time-out," he said with a shaky laugh, and she looked at him in wonder, amazed that she could stir him so. Her eyes glowed with love, and he reached for her again. This time the feather-light touch of his lips moved delicately across her forehead. When he pulled away, she traced the line of his jaw with one fingertip, still finding it hard to believe that she was really in his arms.

"You bring a part of me to life that I never even knew existed," she whispered.

"And you brought a part of me *back* to life," he said quietly.

"Oh, Jeremy, I love you so!"

He leaned back and cupped her face tenderly in his hands.

"To new beginnings, Casey," he said with a smile, his love clearly and openly reflected in his eyes.

"To new beginnings," she repeated.

Then he drew her close once more, and his kiss was full of sweet promise as his lips claimed hers.